Praise for *The "Crime" of Francis Bacon*:

"In the first half of the 20th century, Francis Bacon served as a heroic figure for people far removed from Renaissance England—and often from Renaissance studies. This admirable book goes some way toward explaining his appeal: Written in the 1950s and unpublished until now, its energy and relevance are undiminished."

—**Professor Bill Sherman**, Director of the Warburg Institute, London

I0528984

THE "CRIME" of FRANCIS BACON

on. Lord
fterwards
llor of
1617

THE "CRIME" of FRANCIS BACON

AN INFORMAL BIOGRAPHY

EDGAR KEMLER

Author of *The Irreverent Mr. Mencken*

MISSION POINT PRESS

Copyright © 2023 Edgar Kemler

No parts of this book may be reproduced, stored in a retrieval system, or
transmitted by any means without written permission from the publisher except in
the case of brief quotations for the purpose of critical articles or reviews.
For information or permission, contact:

Mission Point Press
2554 Chandler Road
Traverse City, Michigan 49696
www.MissionPointPress.com

Printed in the United States of America

ISBN: 978-1-961302-30-3 (softcover)
978-1-961302-32-7 (harcover)

Library of Congress Control Number: 2023921721

MISSION POINT PRESS

CONTENTS

FOREWORD

Alan Stewart, Professor, Columbia University

The typescript of *The "Crime" of Francis Bacon* was almost completed when Edgar Kemler passed away in 1960. If he had lived, there's every chance that it would have soon reached print. And if it had, it would have spearheaded a remarkable slew of American books in the early sixties that took Bacon as their focal point: J. Max Patrick's *Francis Bacon* (1961); Virgil K. Whitaker's *Francis Bacon's Intellectual Milieu* (1962); Loren Eiseley's *Francis Bacon and the Modern Dilemma* (1962); Fulton Anderson's *Francis Bacon, His Career and His Thought* (1962); and Catherine Drinker Bowen's *Francis Bacon: The Temper of a Man* (1963). These studies fall into two camps, either placing Bacon in his historical context, or claiming him as a visionary. *The "Crime" of Francis Bacon* is the rare book that does both.

Kemler knew that his strategy of exploring Bacon's thought through his biography was dangerous, but he determined that "I know of no other way of doing justice to the man." Bacon's life was controversial even while he was still alive—accused of turning on his erstwhile patron, the earl of Essex, and then ruined by charges of taking bribes as a judge. Alexander Pope notoriously condemned him as "the wisest, brightest, meanest of mankind," and subsequent Bacon scholars became mired in a pitched battle for Bacon's reputation. Tracking his subject's life made sense for Kemler, however, because Bacon was "so completely obsessed with his dream of the future that unless this dream is related directly to his actions, his story is almost wholly unintelligible." (Dreams pervade this book—the word occurs some forty times.) Kemler's great achievement is to plot a throughline for the life that bears out that obsession and that dream.

At the heart of Kemler's study lies the question of how government might best support organized research. Bacon's "crime," he suggests, stemmed from the fact that Bacon could not simultaneously serve his government and his own research, a situation that led, inexorably and inevitably, to his devastating fall from grace and office in 1621. Kemler claims to see his subject as neither saint nor sinner, yet his sympathies are clearly with Bacon, as he marvels at how his "indomitable and indestructible" faith in his enterprise led ultimately to a seismic shift in official policy towards science. "How important this change was in the life and well-being of mankind," Kemler insists, "cannot be overestimated."

As we approach the 400th anniversary of his death, Bacon's reputation is again on the rise. New editions of his works are under way in English, French, and Romanian, and there is renewed interest in many of his writings. But judging from the endless commentary it prompts, his most popular text by far is now the *New Atlantis*—the "fable" that introduces the research community of Salomon's House, what Kemler called his "dream of the future." *The "Crime" of Francis Bacon* may be reaching the press sixty years late, but it is now definitively of the moment.

PREFACE

S ome men live ahead of their times; others live behind them. Francis
Bacon, who was born in 1561 near St. Albans, England, lived so
far ahead of his age that we have still not entirely caught up with him.
More than 350 years ago, he foresaw the electric light, the telephone, the
airplane, miracle drugs, and many other inventions that are still in blueprint in the scientists' hope chest.[1] These prophecies, though anticipated
somewhat by his namesake, Roger Bacon, who lived 250 years before him,
were remarkable enough. Yet even more remarkable was Bacon's belief
that with government at his disposal for an organized research effort he
could, at best, invent all of these items in his own time, or at worst, invent
one or two of them. In this conviction, he carved out a political career for
himself. It carried him from a youthful misfit into the office of the Lord
Chancellor, the highest office under King James I. Here he had every
opportunity to put his scheme to the test. But, since the enterprise failed,
since he could not even achieve his minimum objective, he was summarily dismissed from office and spent the last five years of his life in forced
retirement.

Our own wartime experience with the Manhattan Project that produced
the atomic bomb has shown us just what might be expected from such an
enterprise as this—when undertaken under skilled direction and at the right
historical moment. But in that remote day, the whole scheme was so novel

---

1   The actual time since the prophecies of Francis Bacon is more than four hundred
years ago. This book was written in the late 1950s.

that few of Bacon's contemporaries had any idea what he was up to. They charged him with corruption in his administration of the Court of Chancery. Bacon freely confessed his guilt on this score. But the record shows that it was his servants, not Bacon, who actually performed the illegal acts, while Bacon merely neglected to punish them quickly enough. In explaining this neglect, Bacon indicated that his mind was occupied elsewhere, namely, in his futile efforts at "the invention of all things possible." Nor can there be any doubt that this was indeed the case. Yet, whatever the explanation, clearly Bacon was not properly discharging the duties of his high office. And however excessive his punishment may have been, certainly his dismissal from office was justified.

This, in brief, was Bacon's "crime," and had the matter ended there, he would have gone down once and for all time as a discredited politician and a discredited miracle worker. Yet his faith in his enterprise was indomitable and indestructible. Through the books that stemmed from it, *The Advancement of Learning* and the *New Machine* (*Novum Organum*), he ignited a bonfire in the best minds of his time. Through these disciples and their successors, the official policy towards science was gradually changed. How important this change was in the life and well-being of mankind cannot be overestimated. Before Bacon, it was generally held that scientific research was impractical, irreverent, and irreligious. (Indeed, had not this misunderstanding been so widespread, Bacon, perhaps, would never have assumed his political guise in the first place.) After Bacon, the approach was just the opposite. If research today is not regarded as the noblest of all human endeavors (as Bacon would have it), it is certainly known to be the most profitable. It was almost as though some higher destiny had deliberately deluded this man and marked him for destruction so that the great inventions he dreamed about would not be lost because of blind policies.

If this interpretation of the man is correct, then we may assess him in a somewhat different light than before. Hitherto, there have been two conflicting schools of thought about Bacon. The one school headed by the great essayist Macaulay held that Bacon was a toady, a blackguard, and a corruptionist; the other school, following James Spedding, who devoted a lifetime of study to the subject, held that Bacon was a highly moral man, except for a certain carelessness in his financial dealings. In the 19th century, these two schools fought each other into a deadlock so complete that relatively little has been written about the man since then. (It was because of this deadlock, I suspect, that the myth of Bacon as the author of Shakespeare's plays first gained currency.) As I see him, he was neither wholly a saint nor wholly a sinner, but an integrated combination of the two. For it was his frustration as a saint that led directly to his transformation into a sinner.

Such titans as this are very rare. His closest parallel, I think, is the titan Prometheus, who stole fire from the gods to confer it upon mankind, and who also was punished for his "crime." Bacon was uniquely the product of the violent, titanic age of Elizabeth I. However, if the world had learned something from its experience with the first Bacon, that is to say, if the world had consistently followed an enlightened policy towards its scientists, on the one hand, and its poets and dreamers, on the other, there would be no need for a second Bacon today. This does not mean that the world must necessarily coddle its dreamers and vest them with supreme political power. We have only recently learned the dangers of excessive idealism in high places in our own government.[2] But we forget that there is an even greater danger in condemning and ignoring idealists because of a misguided handful. We forget how often the "impossible" schemes and dreams of yesterday become the political necessities of today, as was the case with Bacon. Even if they do nothing more than keep the faith that Bacon gave them— the faith in the high destiny of mankind—they earn their keep. For without such a faith, all other striving tends to be chaotic and meaningless, and perhaps also, ill-fated.

The story of Bacon's war with his contemporaries has been told often enough. But certainly it has never been spelled out chapter by chapter in the terms stated above. This is not because of any love of novelty on my part. It is rather because I know of no other way of doing justice to the man. Bacon was so completely obsessed with his dream of the future that unless

2   The author may be referring to the period of the New Deal in the 1930s. Edgar Kemler authored the book, *The Deflation of American Ideals: An Ethical Guide for New Dealers* in 1941.

this dream is related directly to his actions, his story is almost wholly unin-telligible. Inevitably, there is risk in this kind of portraiture. Here and there in his letters and his autobiographical writings, Bacon gives us the key to his obsessions. But there are also moments when he seems to have lost control over himself, and the writer has to supply the missing key by conjecture out of statements in another context. Yet such conjectures are justified, I believe, if they are clearly labelled for what they are, and if they add up to a plausi-ble portrait.

This portrait is based in large part on the original source materials collected by James Spedding in his monumental, seven-volume *Letters and Life* (1861–74) and in the *Collected Works* edited by Spedding, Robert Leslie Ellis, and Douglas Heath, also in seven volumes (1857–59). For intimate biographical detail, I have relied most heavily on the works of Bacon's contemporaries or near-contemporaries. Most notable of these are *Resuscitio* by Dr. William Rawley (London, W. Leed, 1671), *Baconiana* by Archbishop Tenison (London, Richard Chiswell, 1679) and *Brief Lives* by John Aubrey, edited by Andrew Clark (Oxford, Clarendon Press, 1898). For historical background I have consulted J. E. Neale's excellent *Queen Elizabeth* (London, Jonathan Cape, 1934) and Samuel R. Gardiner's classic *History of England 1603–1642*, Vols. I, II, and III (London, Longmans, Green, 1900). For general scientific and philosophical background, I have referred most frequently to A. Wolfe's *A History of Science, Technology and Philosophy in the 16th and 17th Centuries* (New York, Macmillan, 1935). I have also examined the unpublished letters of Sir Thomas Bodley to Bacon in the New York Public Library, and one of them is printed here for the first time.

Other books that I have made use of and that shed light either on Bacon himself, his contemporaries, or on his times are as follows:

Abbott, E. A. *Bacon and Essex* (London, 1877)
———. *Bacon, an Account of his Life and Works* (London, 1885)
Anderson, Fulton, *The Philosophy of Francis Bacon* (Chicago, Univ of Chicago Press, 1948)
Butterfield, Herbert, *The Origins of Science* (London, Bell, 1949)
Byrne, M. St. Clare, *Elizabethan Life in Town and Country* (London, Methuen, 1925)

Church, R. W., *Bacon* in English Man of Letters Series (London, 1884)

Chute, Marchette, *Shakespeare of London* (New York, E.P. Dutton, 1949)

Dennis, G. Ravencroft, *The Cecil Family* (Boston, Houghton, Mifflin Co., 1914)

D'Ewes, Sir Simonds, *The Autobiography and Correspondence of Sir Simonds d'Ewes, Bart, Vol. 1 of 2: During the Reigns of James I. and Charles I.* (London, Richard Bentley, 1845)

Anonymous, *The Secret History of the Reign of James I* (in the same Volume as above)

Farrington, Benjamin, *Bacon, Philosopher of Industrial Science* (New York, Henry Schumann, Inc. 1949)

Gough, J. W., *The Superlative Prodigall: A Life of Thomas Bushell* (Bristol, J. W. Arrowsmith, 1932)

Green, A. W., *Sir Francis Bacon, His Life and Works* (Denver, Allen Swallow, 1952)

Hervey, Mary, *The Earl of Arundel* (Cambridge Univ. Press, 1921)

Lee, Sir Sidney, *A Life of William Shakespeare* (New York, Macmillan Co., 1916)

Lyon, Hastings and Block, Herman, *Edward Coke* (New York, 1929)

Macauley, Thomas B., *Essays and Poems*, Vol. II (New York, American Book Exchange, 1880)

Mackay, Charles, *Extraordinary Popular Delusions and the Madness of Crowds* (Boston, L. C. Page, 1932)

Maitland, William, *The History of London to the Present Time* (London, 1739)

Mathew, A. H., *The Life of Sir Tobie Matthew* (London, Elkin Mathews, 1907)

Raleigh, Walter, *Shakespeare's England* (2 vols) (Oxford, Clarendon Press, 1917)

Reese, M. M., *The Tudors and Stuarts* (London, Edward Arnold, 1940)

Seegmuller, Francis, *Francis Bacon* (New York, Doubleday, Doran, 1930)

Smeeton's *Historical and Biographical Tracts* (Westminster, 1820)

Sorley, W. A., *A History of English Philosophy* (Cambridge University Press, 1937)

Stebbing, Williams, *Sir Walter Raleigh* (Oxford, Clarendon Press, 1891)

Steeholms, Clara and Hardy, *James I of England* (New York Covici Friede, 1938)

Stimson, Dorothy, *Scientists and Amateurs: The Royal Society* (New York, Henry Schuman, 1948)

Strachey, Lytton, *Elizabeth and Essex* (London, Chatto and Windus, 1928)

Sturt, Mary, *Francis Bacon* (London, 1932)

Taylor, F Sherwood, *The Alchemists* (New York, Henry Schuman, 1949)

Trevelyan, G. M., *England Under the Stuarts* (London, Methuen, 1904)

———. *English Social History* (London, Longmans Green, 1942)

Willey, Basil, *The 17th Century Background* (London, Chatto and Windus, 1949)

Wilson, A, *History of Great Britain, the Life and Reign of James I* (London, 1653)

Winwood, Sir Ralph, *Memorials of Affairs of State in the Reigns of Elizabeth and James I*

THE "CRIME" of FRANCIS BACON

CHAPTER ONE

THE MIRACLE THAT PHIZZED

"A sound magician is a mighty God."
— *Marlowe, Dr. Faustus*

One bright day either in 1582 or '83, two young law students from Gray's Inn hastened along Thames Street to London Bridge. A mixed crowd of beggars and apprentices had already gathered on the approaches of the bridge. The Lord Mayor and the aldermen were expected imminently. It was a festive occasion—the official opening of the new pumping station that had been installed under one of the arches of the bridge. It was also historic, for this "curious machine" as it was called, was the first of its kind in England, the 100,000-odd Londoners having depended hitherto on a primitive system of wells and pipes from springs. Designed by Peter Maurice, German engineer, the pumping station was a two-storey affair, with crude pump, piston, and cams in the upper storey. On the lower storey was the power unit, which consisted of two horses walking endlessly round and round against a drive shaft.

When the Mayor and aldermen made their approach, the horses were whipped into motion for the first time. There was an ominous pause, while the pistons sucked and the valves clicked in the pipelines. Then a great shout went up from the assembled throng. From the free end of an upright pipe the water shot over St. Magnus' steeple (more than 60 feet high)—"before which time," a contemporary wrote, "no such thing was known in England as this raising of water."

The two students had arrived just in time to witness this performance. But instead of cheering with the others, they stood apart to discuss its long-range implications. This is a beginning, said Francis Bacon to his companion, but just a beginning. These "marvels" of the engineers are really "gross inventions that lie not far out of the way" from what the ancients have done. Compared to the great scientific revolution that he was then revolving in his mind, he went on, this affair will hardly be noticed by future historians. Indeed, when this second revolution was consummate (and he did not think it would take long), there would be no need for pumping stations. The water could be collected directly from clouds. Also, by some device which admittedly he could not foresee, the sun would shine over the city by night as well as by day, and instead of racing through the muddy streets, he and his companion could fly through the air like a couple of swallows.

The 21-year-old Bacon was of middle height, with a dark beard after the fashion of the time, running full circle from the upper lip to the chin, and with no noteworthy features save for his remarkable hazel eyes. The folds around them were puffy from too much reading under a guttering lamp. But the eyes themselves were as clear and lucid as cathedral windows. Had his companion looked deep enough into them, he could have seen there the very essence of the man. For this man, who could see, in his own words, "to the bottom of the sea," and perhaps, as far into the future destiny of mankind as any man has ever seen, was also almost totally blind both as to the limitations of his contemporaries and of himself.

Dr. William Rawley, one of Bacon's later disciples, tells us that his revelations came not from the many books that he read, "but from some grounds and notions within himself." "If ever there were an original thinker," he wrote, "if ever there were a beam of knowledge derived from God upon any man in these modern times [i.e. Bacon's times], it was upon him." True enough. However, for every great dream, there is always an actual touchstone. What this touchstone was in Bacon's case, how or when he stumbled upon it, we don't know.

However, from the evidence now in hand, it was probably in 1575, when he was 14, just before he left Cambridge University. One of the private tutors in his father's household was an astronomer, Leonard Digges.

Digges owned a proportional glass "or telescope with which he could read the inscription on a coin at a considerable distance, spy out lovers in a wood 7 miles away and detonate a load of gunpowder at 1 ½ miles or further." For most people, the telescope was a mere toy, but for the imaginative Bacon, it must have had colossal implications. If the power of the naked eye could thus be multiplied many times, he asked why couldn't the other senses be likewise enhanced—the ear, for example?

One of the pillars in his little room at Trinity College was hollow: by pressing his ear close to it, he could hear conversation clearly in another room some distance off. This suggested that the human voice could be "amplified, distorted, analyzed, and carried through pipes long distance" by what we call a telephone. At the same time, no doubt, other accidents of nature had attracted his attention and these suggested other inventions. The "quick ripening of grapes" in the back of chimneys suggested hothouses; phosphorescence of one kind or another suggested electric lights, or "divers means of producing light originally from diverse bodies"; the flight of birds suggested "some degrees of human flying in the air," or airplanes. Then, perhaps, he reflected on the Great Plague that had caused the Universities to shut down for six months during that very year. There was some connection, it was believed, between the plague and the extreme dampness of the air. If the plague itself could not be cured, Bacon asked, why could not something be done about the air, something like modern weather control?

It was so easy for him to imagine these new inventions that it seemed almost equally easy for him actually to invent them. Here in nature, just beyond the range of ordinary vision, was an empire richer than all Spanish possessions of the New World, richer than anything that had been imagined before. "Kings with their treasure can not buy [this empire] nor with their force command it; their spies and intelligencies can give no news of [it]; their seamen and discoverers cannot sail where it [flourishes]."[3] By virtue of his intimate "conversation with nature," he and he alone had access to this new empire; that is to say, he was its potential conqueror.

---

3   The author Edgar Kemler, in making assumptions about what Bacon intended, added his own words in brackets. Elsewhere, including in the following paragraph, Kemler added clarifying text in parentheses. The editors decided to leave Kemler's markings as he wrote them in his original manuscript. Throughout the text, the editorial team made judgment calls to ensure readability while honoring the author's original wording.

But if only his contemporaries would cooperate with him in a large-scale research enterprise, which consisted largely of an inventory of all "natural phenomena of heavenly bodies, meteors, earth and sea," he would share it with them either in part or in whole. Hitherto all the great inventions had been "more or less stumbled upon by chance" (he mentioned the compass, gunpowder, and printing as the chief examples). But by his enterprise, "whole troops of inventions" would be forthcoming, and they would come, "not one here and one there, but in clusters."

Had this enterprise worked the way he said it would, by the end of this book he would have been a conqueror, indeed, and could have dominated his age as no man has ever dominated any age. By his patent rights, he could have made himself as rich as Croesus. By his powers of prophecy, or of "natural divination" as it was then called, he could have been the bellwether of the stock exchange. By his exclusive control over the instruments of "war and poison," he could have brandished a club over his government. However, Bacon tells us he was not concerned about material rewards and that he would have made all, or almost all, his inventions freely available to the public. Thereby the standard of living would have been raised as high above the existing level "in the most polished countries of Europe," as this, in turn, was above that of "any wild and barbarous region of the Indies." "To look for any private gain from such an undertaking as this, I consider both ridiculous and base."

The enterprise itself was so challenging and absorbing that it "may well be content with its own merit without seeking other compensation."

Superficially, this enterprise of Bacon's was plausible enough—a prototype of the great research establishment that we have today. But, as he later demonstrated, it was only a philosopher's dream castle, or conversely a scientist's nightmare, with every detail of the operation distorted and with a timetable of research so ambitious that, in short order, it would have laid all his assistants low with nervous breakdowns (as it very nearly did). Yet for all that, it would fill a great historical need. For one thing, it would serve as a kind of showpiece by which Bacon could advertise the great new era that would result if only his government would give official recognition to research. For another thing, it would be a useful literary weapon for shaming the enemies of science and rallying its friends.

At times, Bacon seems to have understood the strange role that destiny had assigned him. "If a man could strike a light unto all ages," he wrote, "a light which would ultimately disclose all that is most hidden and secret in the world, that man would, indeed, be the benefactor of the human race." Yet luckily for us, he would never understand his personal limitations. For had he not believed that he could actually invent "all things possible," he could never have taken the colossal risks nor faced up to the constant rebuffs that were inevitable in his mission. In his youth, he not merely believed all this, but also believed that by merely announcing his "true" identity, the whole machinery of the English government would be made available to him.

�֎

In the first place, according to his calculations, no government could co-operate properly in his enterprise until it had established the proper conditions. These were: (1) an era of peace and prosperity, (2) a settlement of religious squabbles, (3) "the open traffic of the globe, both by sea and land"; and (4) the cultivation of genius.

Bacon was born on January 22, 1561, which was in the third year of Queen Elizabeth's reign. At that time, affairs in England were so unsettled that his enterprise would have been unthinkable. But by the time of his majority, Elizabeth had gone so far to meet these conditions that it seemed as though she had consciously worked to set the stage for him.

With a minimum of expense and a relatively small show of military force, she had won the respect of both Spain and France, each four times as populous as little England. At the same time, by well-calculated measures of internal economy, such as the encouragement of immigration and home industry, she had so increased the national wealth that there was plenty available for him (or so Bacon thought). Through her admirals, merchants, and privateers (Bacon was 10 when Drake completed the circumnavigation of the globe in the record-breaking time of two years and ten months), she had established that "open traffic of the globe" whence we receive "numerous experiments unknown to former ages and many [new] natural objects fit to throw light upon the sciences." Through the re-establishment of the Church of England, she had momentarily settled the religious strife that had occupied the best minds under her two predecessors, and left them free for more worldly and hence more important problems. Finally, through her manifest glory, she had inspired (or soon would) her poets to the greatest outburst of song the world has ever seen and heard. And if Bacon could somehow redirect their creative energies from flights of fancy to the empire of nature, he would have a truly gifted body of researchers at his disposal.

In the second place, he knew (or soon learned) that to gain support for such a novel enterprise as this, he would have to gain access to the Queen and her Privy Council. Here again, fortune favored him. His father was Sir Nicholas Bacon, the Lord Keeper, and perhaps the third most important of the Queen's councillors while his uncle, William Cecil—Lord Burghley— was generally acknowledged to be the chief architect of her "happy reign." These two men were the leaders of a new party in English public life—a party of "new men," strongly Protestant and militantly aggressive vis-à-vis Spain. Their ascendancy coincided with the decline of the old pro-Catholic, pro-Spanish lords. Two years before Bacon's birth, they broke a conspiracy of these lords which might otherwise have cost them their lives. After Bacon's birth, their position was somewhat more secure, but still exciting enough. And since the turbulence of the court had its repercussions in the Bacon household, Bacon learned about politics at a very early age indeed.

When things were going well at court, the Queen would come to visit Sir Nicholas either at York House, his London palace, or at his country manor at Gorhambury. Once on a visit to the latter place, the Queen made sport of her Lord Keeper for its modesty. "My Lord, what a little house you have gotten," she exclaimed.

"Madam," replied Sir Nicholas, ponderously, "my house is well, but it is you that have made me too great for my house." On the other hand, when things went badly at court, and Sir Nicholas was temporarily refused access to the Queen's presence chamber, the Bacon household became a court in exile. When Bacon was three, for example, Sir Nicholas was banished for having written an anonymous pamphlet on the royal succession. Bacon's mother then cheered her husband with wise words and otherwise played "a good wife's part," reading aloud to him out of the classics. One of the four daughters of the scholar Sir Anthony Cook, Lady Anne Bacon was in her own right a very cultivated person, known as a writer and translator.

Sir Nicholas had eight children, six of whom were by a previous wife, two, Anthony and Francis, by Lady Anne, the second wife. Of all these children, Sir Nicholas liked Francis best and regarded him as the most likely prospect for a great career at court. But in this the old man was mistaken. During his nonage, Francis was trained by private tutors; at 12, which was young, but not exceptionally so, he was enrolled at Trinity College, Cambridge; at 15, he was apprenticed to Sir Amias Paulet, the English ambassador in Paris. In each case, he responded well to his training; at the end of his apprenticeship in Paris, Sir Amias even gave him a certificate of merit. But his performance did not match his high promise and by his own admission at this time he was "not greatly perfect in the ceremonies of the court." It was not that he lacked ambition (far from it), but rather that he was not temperamentally suited to court life. He was shy, retiring—what we would call introspective. He preferred to speculate in the "naked and open daylight" of the Gorhambury countryside rather than to take part in the "masques and mummeries and triumphs" of the London court.

Meanwhile, at 14 or thereabouts, he discovered what he took as his true identity as the potential conqueror of nature. In a flash the root of his difficulty was revealed to him. Why, indeed, should he be preparing himself for the court, when the court should be preparing itself for him? And as soon as he had explained to his father and his Uncle Burghley what great things he had in store for them, no doubt they would do this. On this assumption, at any rate, he willfully neglected his studies. All other ambition seemed "poor in my eye," he tells us, seeing that "the matter at issue" was either nothing or everything. At Cambridge, as noted above, he commenced work on his telephone by experiments with the defective pillar. In Paris, he continued this work by studying the echoes in caves. Meanwhile, everywhere he went he announced the advent of the "empire of nature." Some men were much taken with him. After a couple of sittings with him, Sir Nicholas Hilliard, the Queen's portrait painter exclaimed, "If one could but paint his mind!" Other men reacted the other way, declaring him to be impossibly whimsical and vainglorious.

During his third year in Paris in January 1579, when he was just 18, his father died of a "winter cold" and his Uncle Burghley informed him that it was time to get on with the next stage in his education. This was his legal training at Gray's Inn where his father had already had him enrolled. But by this time, he thought he was ready to come into his own. "The practice of law," he protested, was a kind of refuge for "the poor and the friendless."

Nobody who had a chance of "likely success" with other studies "of more delight and no less preferment" would ever "fall in with" it of his own "free election," etc., etc. How Bacon's father would have reacted to this declaration is difficult to say. He had always been very indulgent of his favorite son. Yet through some unexplained oversight in the drafting of his will, Bacon was left less than one-fifth of his rightful inheritance. For the time being, he was more or less dependent on his Uncle Burghley and the latter was extremely skeptical about his talk of "industrious observations, grounded conclusions, and profitable inventions and discoveries." Thus, before he knew it, Bacon found himself studying law at Gray's Inn, like any other "poor and friendless" student.

✳

In the course of his astonishing career, this would-be conqueror of nature would be very grateful to his uncle for this decision. For without a solid profession such as the law to fall back on, his dreams might have been stillborn and he might never have struck his light at all. Yet at the moment he was annoyed with his uncle. Law repelled him not only as a profession but as a study. It was a disorderly and vague mass of statutes and precedents, some of which were obsolete and some still in force. Worse yet, the law books themselves were badly written, "being too verbose and prolix." Yet, by a scientific system of memory training, which he now developed for this purpose, he mastered the law in four years instead of the usual five, becoming an utter barrister in June 1582, and a bencher in 1586. Later, when a readership was conferred upon him, he lectured to his colleagues on how the common law could be reformed and reorganized on scientific principles—a suggestion that has recently been adopted in both England and America[4]—and thus took his revenge on the profession that he hated. At any rate, when he had completed his training, he appealed a second time to Burghley, "the Atlas of

---

4 The author may have been referring to the 1950s work of Friedrich Hayek and Bruno Leoni, free-market philosophers who suggested that common law naturally evolves, whereas laws passed by legislative bodies are arbitrarily made. Reference "The Evolution of Common Law" by Gennaioli and Shleifer, *Journal of Political Economy*, 2007, vol 115, no. 1.

this commonwealth, the honor of my house, and the second founder of my poor estate" to help him with the "orderly" conquest of nature.

Now, just to attract attention to his enterprise, the young Bacon did something very bold, and also very foolish. He set himself up in competition with alchemists, astrologers, and other quacks, declaring that he could do in fact what they only pretended to do. From time immemorial, these people had occupied a place in the antechambers of Kings and Queens and, if nothing else, had kept their clients diverted with their marvelous claims. Alchemists claimed the secret of eternal life and quick riches by the conversion of lead to gold; astrologers claimed knowledge of the future, while sorcerers supposedly maintained communications with the spirit world. The Elizabethan court seems to have been more skeptical of these people than the other courts of Europe, though even here, they had their devotees. For there were very clever imposters among them, and as soon as one was exposed and discredited, another would rise in his stead. In later life, Bacon would deplore "the great prejudice" that he had incurred in his own enterprise because of "the imposters who had made similar attempts" in this field—a prejudice, he said, that was almost overpowering. But in his youth, at any rate, there can be doubt but that he deliberately invited this prejudice.

At this very time, one of these imposters was enjoying great vogue both in Queen Elizabeth's court and among foreign royalty. He was Dr. John Dee. After an uncertain beginning and a brief term in prison for using sorcery against Elizabeth's predecessor, Queen "Bloody" Mary, he had made his first impression at court by picking the lucky day for the new Queen's coronation. Encouraged by this success, he had moved step-by-step into the higher forms of quackery. In 1581, he had acquired a semi-transparent crystal ball by which he and his assistant, the one-time forger, Dr. Kelly, claimed they could communicate with the dead. In 1585, in the midst of a visit with the Holy Roman Emperor, he announced that he had found the long sought method of transmuting lead into gold.

At first, it looked as though Dr. Dee had overreached himself. The court was divided in its reaction to his supposed discovery. One faction of skeptics said "they would not believe it unless they could see it." Another faction, headed by the Archbishop of Canterbury, accepted the testimony of a new traveler who said that he had actually seen it. The Queen's diplomatic correspondence, unearthed by modern scholars, reveals that neither the Queen nor her loyal Burghley was taken in by this quack and that by sending him abroad, they were simply using him to pry out the secrets of rival powers. Bacon, apparently, did not know this. And in his every appearance before the court, he presented his claims against those of Dr. Dee and his ilk.

The most dramatic and ingenious of these presentations occurred in 1594 at the annual Christmas frolic of Gray's Inn before a distinguished audience of privy councillors, including his Uncle Burghley. Every year, it seems, the students and barristers here took advantage of Yuletide cheer to poke some good-natured fun at the Queen and her court. The revelers put on the robes of high functionaries, exchanged "ambassadors" with the other Inns of Court and then, intermittently from Christmas day to Twelfth Night, produced masques or playlets, burlesquing the passing scene. On the second night of the revel, there was an unrehearsed mix-up. "A company of base and common fellowes" burst into the hall, crowded the actors off the stage and threw the "court" into "confusion and errors." Resuming the burlesque, the next night an inquest was held into this "night of errors." A certain "sorceror or conjuror" (Dr. Dee?) was named as the cause of that "confused inconvenience" along with certain "privy councillors" who had encouraged him. After the latter had been "tried," "convicted," and "sent" to the Tower, a new set of "councillors" was installed to preside over the revels—young men of "graver conceit," including Bacon himself. A few days later, Bacon exploited this symbolic victory over the sorcerer, Dr. Dee, to beat a drum for his own enterprise.

Speaking through a "privy councillor" in a masque written and produced by himself, he urged the Queen to devote her whole strength to "the most innocent and meriting conquest—the conquest of the works of nature—the searching out, inventing, and discovering of all whatsoever is hid and secret in the world." To this end he suggested four principal installations: first, a perfect library, "wherein whatsoever the wit of man hath hitherto committed to books of worth"; second, a complete herborarum, "wherein whatsoever plant the sun of divers climates either wild or by the culture of man hath brought forth may be set and cherished," and a complete zoo with "rooms to stable in all rare beasts"; third, a technological museum; and finally, a "still house," or chemical laboratory, "so furnished with mills, instruments, furnaces and vessels as it may be a place fit for [organized research]."

From a practical viewpoint, Bacon may have recalled that the Queen had already started the zoo with certain rooms in the Tower of London where six-legged calves and other monstrosities were on display. Also, he may have noted that she had helped Dr. Dee to set up a laboratory at Mortlake—a laboratory for quackery that might easily be confiscated and adapted to his enterprise. At any rate, this was not intended merely as a prophecy of things to come, but rather as a working blueprint of the research college by which, he believed, his extravagant claims would be vindicated. With such a college, he suggested, and under his direction, Your Majesty shall be a "Trismegistus," the sorcerer of sorcerers. "Then all other [phony] miracles and wonders shall cease by reason that you shall have discovered their natural causes, and yourself shall be left the only miracle and wonder of the world." Later, Bacon went even further than this. Not only would his enterprise discredit the imposters, he wrote, but it would soon perform, in fact, most of the miracles that these quacks only pretended to perform—and hundreds of others besides, much more remarkable.

Did the imposters claim to predict men's future from the position of the star? He could really do this, if only he knew the effects of the stars on the weather, of the weather on plagues, epidemics, and famines, and of the latter on war, seditions, migrations of people, etc. Did they claim to convert lead into gold? Wisely, he would not commit himself to this. But if it could be done at all, he wrote, it could be done better by a "man acquainted with all the principles of metals" than by one who knows but "the bare projection of a few grains of magic powder." He made the same conjecture about the prolongation of life. "It may be more rationally done by diet, regimen of health, baths, and medicines directed by accurate knowledge of the human frame than by a few drops of some precious liquor." Yet the difficulty of his position was this: Without such a research college as he had described in his masque, he could give no proofs of these miracles. But without proofs, his Uncle Burghley would applaud the "manner" of his appeals, which was exquisite, but ignore the "matter." In any case, before he could bring this college actively into the miracle business, certain preliminary studies had to be made and in the course of these studies, it was possible that he might come up with a sample invention or two. For once "this mine of truth" is opened up, he wrote later, "who can tell how the veins go and what lieth higher and what lieth lower?"

As early as 1582, after the completion of his legal training, he had converted his rooms at Gray's Inn into a small-scale college for these studies. Not much is known about this little college. According to one of his later disciples, whose testimony was not very reliable, his equipment consisted of "a great secret curiosity whereby we know the season of every hour of the year," that is, a water barometer, and an astronomical mock-up representing by wires "the motion of some planets, in fact, as it is." Also from his parental estate at Gorhambury, his mother sent him a picture of an "ancient, learned philosopher," probably the Roman Seneca, whom he regarded as his close forerunner in the ancient world.

His laboratory assistants and gentleman attendants were chosen from among the most promising graduates of Oxford and Cambridge, the most important of whom was Tobie Matthew. "A very worthy and rare young gentleman," the son of the Bishop of Norwich, Bacon sometimes referred to him as his "alter ego," and did many services for him, as we shall see in due course. In his turn, Matthew served Bacon in the Christmas masques that he wrote, later as a fellow legislator in Parliament, and at all times as a sounding board for his meditations. In conversation with him, Bacon "tosseth his thoughts more easily," "marshalleth them more orderly," and generally "waxeth wiser than himself"—and this "more by an hour's discourse than by a day's meditation [by himself]."

Carefully, Bacon kept notes on all his experiments (though few of these have survived), and in its later forms, this model college would become the prototype of all organized research. Yet from an administrative standpoint it was ill-managed and ill-fated. Bacon puttered about with his instruments all afternoon, all evening, and far into the night, as his mother said, "musing I know not what when he should sleep." The next morning he rose late— a regimen his mother went on to describe as, "whereby his men are made slothful and himself continually sick." His funds were kept in a chest drawer without lock or key; no ledger was kept, or if it was kept, it was not kept current, so when his men wanted extra pin money they would simply scoop out as much as they needed without fear of detection.

By his rule of thumb, "his ordinary expenses ought to be put to the half of his receipts," or better yet, to the "third part." But he could not muster the courage to look into his estate, "doubting to bring himself into melancholy in respect he shall find it broken," and since he had no regular income, his fears on this score were justified. True, his reputation as a legal scholar was so great that he could easily have replenished his exchequer by legal practice. But he would not spare the time for this. Whenever his money drawer was empty, he simply applied to Burghley for a loan. If only he could get his enterprise to bear fruit in its present form, he hinted, he would more than repay his uncle with "works of power and utility."

Meanwhile, Bacon's model college had aroused adverse comment at court. Since pride and arrogance were now habitual with him, his public relations soon became something of a problem. One day, Nicholas Faunt, a friend of Bacon's brother Anthony, and a highly placed bore, paid a visit to Bacon's headquarters in Gray's Inn. Anthony was then travelling on official business on the continent, and Faunt wanted to exchange news with Francis about him. He was met in an outer hall by one of Francis' servants. Mister Bacon was not then at leisure to receive Mister Faunt, said the servant, having just returned from Gorhambury and being fully occupied in important business of his own. Would Mister Faunt care to leave a message? Faunt was much too skilled a courtier to confide what he had to say through a servant. But in his next letter to Anthony, he complained of "this strangeness which hath at [this and] other times been used towards me by your brother."

Since this same strangeness had already been noted by others, many damaging rumors were now circulated about Bacon, until one day in 1585, Burghley called on the youngster to account for them. Bacon's reply was prompt. "In my simple observation" he wrote, "I find that they which live as it were in the shade and not in public or frequent action, how moderately and modestly soever they behave themselves, yet labor under spite. I find also that such persons as are of nature bashful (as myself is), whereby they want that plausible familiarity which others have, are often mistaken for proud." However, since Bacon believed his own work to be so much more important than Burghley's, there could be no question about his pride. As the years went by, this fault became worse rather than better. The ancients, he noted later, "numbered the authors of rude [unscientific] inventions among the gods. For it was plain [to them] that the good effects wrought by [statesmen] last but short times, whereas the work of the inventor, though a thing of less pomp and show, is felt everywhere and lasts forever."

Thus for more than a decade he labored. But after all this time, he still had made no invention nor come up with any proof for his enterprise comparable to Dr. Dee's "proof" of quackery. Worse yet, he had not even collected his thoughts sufficiently to write a coherent prospectus about it, though about 1586 he had attempted such a work under the tentative title, *The Greatest Birth of Time*. One can imagine him, during this period, chasing up all sorts of blind alleys, mixing acid solutions, blowing up retorts, and speculating on how it would all turn out. Yet he was satisfied that his time had not been wasted. Though his enterprise was obviously more "arduous" and its success more "remote" than he had originally thought, he was more convinced of its soundness than ever. "Though success is indeed more pleasing," he wrote later, "yet failure frequently is no less informing," and in this planning stage "experiments of light are more to be desired than experiments of profit."

A further guarantee of its ultimate success was the enthusiasm of his disciples. For if he failed to get it working in his time, he would count on them, or rather on others like them, to do so in the next age. Even at this early date, while he was still so empty-handed, his brother Anthony believed that he had already contributed so "many good things for the general [welfare]" that no reward was adequate for his compensation. The men of Gray's Inn later testified that by setting his headquarters in their midst, he had made them as "third persons with the Nobility and Court in doing the [Crown] honor" and that he had made Gray's Inn flourish "by countenancing virtue" in every class, an allusion to his lack of social snobbery in the selection of his assistants.

❧

In 1592, Bacon was so far gone in debt that once more he had to appeal to Burghley for help. But this time, in view of his failure to provide proof for his enterprise, he did not promise to repay him by inventions, or certainly not by inventions alone, but by regular government service "in some middle place that I could discharge." "I wax now somewhat ancient," he wrote. "One and thirty years is a great deal of sand in the hour glass. My health, I thank God, I find confirmed. And I do not fear that action shall impair it, because I account my ordinary course of study and meditation to be more painful than most parts of action are. [Finally,] I ever bare a mind to serve her Majesty, not for the honor of it, or for the love of it, ("for the

contemplative planet carrieth me away wholly"), but because so excellent
a sovereign 'deserveth the dedication of all men's abilities.'" Yet in making
this appeal, he did not deny that the conquest of nature was still his main
concern. "I have as vast contemplative ends as I have moderate civil ends."
Nor did he deny that once in office he would continue working towards
these ends. For such an office would bring "commandment of more wits
than of a man's own, which is the thing I greatly affect. This, whether it
be curiosity, or vain glory, or [insanity] or (if one take it favorably) philan-
thropy, is so fixed in my mind as it cannot be removed."

At first glance, this would seem to have been a graceful retreat from
his intolerable posture of the previous decade. Yet while partly lowering his
pretensions on one front he vastly raised them on another, as an expert on
government and a "champion of liberty." Asking his uncle for this "middle
place" he had written: "Perhaps your Lordship shall not find more strength
and less encounter [insubordination] in any other public servant." Yet in administrative work he had had very little experience, while in legislative work
(he had first been elected to Parliament in 1584 at the age of 23), he now
put on a performance that showed just how insubordinate he could be. The
Queen had summoned a new Parliament to provide against the threat of a
second Spanish Armada. Only five years had passed since her gallant Navy
had driven off the first Armada; the appropriations demanded by the defence were extraordinarily large; and in her anxiety to get them, the Queen
in league with her privy councillor and the House of Lords, attempted to
suspend the traditional liberties of the House of Commons. Bacon agreed
with the Queen on the justice of the appropriations, but he could not see
that this emergency, or perhaps any emergency, justified such tyrannical tactics. After all, the right of dissent was a *sine qua non* of the great enterprise to
which he had dedicated his life. It was equally important, he thought, in the
deliberations of any government with which he was associated.

Thus, when the Lords threatened to take over initiative from the Commons in the framing of the bill, he urged the Commons to "stand upon their
privilege." "For the custom of this House hath always been first to make
offer of the [bill], which then went from hence unto the Upper House."
After the bill was framed, he made a second objection, urging that it be
amended so that the tax burden would not weigh so heavily on the poor.
"The gentlemen must sell their plate and the farmers their brass pots ere this

will be paid. And as for us, we are here to search wounds of the realm and not to skin them over." Yet by such a tax, he went on, "we shall breed discontentment among the people. And [in this time of crisis], her Majesty's safety must consist more in the love of her people than in their wealth."

As yet, Bacon had not exchanged his philosopher's shyness for the glittering manner he would acquire later on. These impassioned lines were spoken with "Panting and labor of breath" and "without any pretense of good fashion"; he "fell upon the main too sudden." Thus while in the first of his objections, he swayed the majority of the house; in the second, he stood as a minority of one. Yet he had caused the Queen and her councillors much embarrassment and forced them part way back to the traditional procedure.

Hitherto the Queen had often admitted him to her presence chamber and had listened tolerantly to his plans for the conquest of nature. But with this latest exhibition, she realized what a truly uncompromising young man he really was, and that if she helped him to materialize his plans there would simply be no living with him. Also, at this awkward hour, the position of Attorney General had become vacant and he had applied for it—a position which, despite his statements to the contrary, was not a "middle place" at all, but a very high one. But the Queen not only refused to listen to his suit, but also refused to see him. For a lesser offense, she said, her father, King Henry VIII, would have banished him from the court permanently. Speaking through Sir Edward Coke, the speaker of the House of Commons, and himself a contender for the Attorney General's place, she told the Commons that they were veritably "a hive of bees, collecting honey for their Queen." "But where the bee sucketh honey, there also the spider draweth his poison." Later in conversation with Essex, her favorite, who was Bacon's patron in this "suit," she made it unmistakably clear that the spider was Mister Bacon.

Under this counter-attack, Bacon not only refused to back down, but also expressed his "marvel" that the Queen and Burghley should have so little understanding of the role of an opposition. To his uncle's charge that he was seeking popularity by playing off the Commons against the Queen, he replied: Nonsense! "I muse what care I should take to please the many, [I] that taketh a course of life to deal with a few." As to the charge of insubordination, his dissent was dictated by "circumstances of time and manner" on Burghley's part. Certainly "variety is allowed in counsel as a discord in music—to make it more perfect." At the same time he was now painfully aware that his emergence as an expert on government had not helped him in his bid for office, which in turn meant that it had not helped him with his main object: the research college. In his perplexity, he now turned to Burghley's son, his first cousin, Sir Robert Cecil, for advice.

Two years younger than Bacon, Sir Robert had also started with a handicap. In his case, it was not a pretension to superhuman powers, but rather a physical deformity—a stunted body and a crooked back. Ordinarily, the Queen demanded comeliness as well as astuteness in her close advisers. So this was no mean affliction. Throughout his career, he would be referred to by friends and foes alike as a "pygmy," "a beagle," or a "crooked" man. "By my soul," said Lord Wemyss on one occasion, "I could not see him in the Privy Council."

"No Marvel," replied the Lord Chamberlain, "being so little."

But as Bacon later wrote, Cecil had turned his defect into a source of strength and so had taken "revenge on nature." Thus while other courtiers brutally mocked him, he was quietly storing up the worldly wisdom that he needed to command their respect. Before he was 30, he was a member of the Privy Council, and acting Secretary of State; by the time of his father's death, he could claim his father's privacy among the Queen's councillors by ability as well as by inheritance.

Attend closely at court, Cecil advised Bacon, "for loss of occasion may do you much harm." Among other things, this meant that Bacon would have to act like a courtier instead of like the inventor of "all things possible"— practice law, and generally prove his qualifications for the office of Attorney General. Bacon followed Cecil's advice, and by the following March had apparently impressed nearly everybody, including Burghley, with his ability. Yet for some reason that he could not fathom, the Queen still withheld the prize. Bacon felt "like a child following a bird, which when he is nearest flieth away and lighteth a little before, and then the child after it again, *ad infinitum*." After the first four months of his suit, he had succeeded in gaining the Queen's pardon and, in part, her championship. She had promised to make her decision the following September. By September, however, all her old grievances had come to the fore again. He might come to the court, he was told, but he would not be granted such near access to her Majesty as formerly. The following January, he had proved his ability as a trial lawyer only to learn the following Easter that his rival, Sir Edward Coke, had

finally beaten him out. Meanwhile, a vacancy had occurred in the lesser office of Solicitor General. Bacon was persuaded to apply for this position as
a kind of consolation prize, but at the same time, he swore that if no decision were forthcoming, "betwixt this and the next term, never to make any
more words of it." When another year passed without a decision, it gradually dawned on Bacon that the consideration that was being given him was
not the ordinary consideration given to the ordinary courtier, but a plot by
the Queen to make him renounce his imperial pretensions once and for all.
As he later put it, "the Queen did make me burn." Moreover, save for Essex
and perhaps one or two others, he decided that not only the Queen, but
the whole court, was party to the plot. It was true, of course, that his Uncle
Burghley had continuously warned him about these pretensions ever since
his father's death.

His mother had seconded this warning. He could expect nothing from
his Uncle Burghley, she had told him, so long "as he continued still the
means of his own great hindrance." Nonetheless, he seems to have been
completely taken aback by this discovery. Now shaking off his newfound
courtliness and reverting once more to his imperial posture, he plainly told
the plotters, one by one, what he thought of them.

Robert Cecil was the chief offender. "I trust on, yet do not smother
what I hear," Bacon told him sardonically. "I do assure you, sir, that by a
wise friend of mine, and not factious towards your Honor, I was told with
asseveration that your Honor was bought by Mr. Coventry [Bacon's rival
for Solicitor General] . . . the truth of which tale I do not believe." Lord
Keeper Puckering had also professed friendship for the would-be conqueror
of nature. Now, Bacon said he was not fit to fill his father's shoes. "There
hath nothing happened to me in the course of my business more contrary
to my expectation than your Lordship's failing me and crossing me now in
the conclusion."

By contrast with these false friends, his little band of disciples in Gray's
Inn had remained as devoted as ever in this difficult period. In his original
suit for office, he had told his uncle, "If your Lordship will not carry me on,
I will not do as Anaxagoras did, who reduced himself with contemplation
unto voluntary poverty. But this I will do: I will sell the inheritance that I
have, and purchase some lease of quick revenue, of some office of gain that
shall be executed by deputy." Thereafter, he would "give over all care of

service," and surrounded by his disciples, would become "some sorry bookmaker, or a true pioneer in that mine of truth which lies so deep." This plan was now revived in more detail. He would go abroad for a time for a rest. Upon his return, he would retire with a couple of disciples to Cambridge University "and there spend my life in my studies and contemplations without looking back." But the Queen would not grant him the passport that he needed to leave the country, nor would she even listen to his revised plans.

In this hour of trial and frustration, Bacon somehow underwent a great personal transformation—a transformation that would guarantee his success in the long run, if not in the short run. What was to be gained by a policy of retreat and retirement, he asked himself. In the first place, it was obvious now that no matter what proofs he might give them, neither his Uncle Burghley nor the Queen would ever support his enterprise. All his plans and blueprints for it would have to be executed by deputy through his disciples in the next age, and thus, might miscarry altogether.

In the second place, almost by definition, a policy of retreat and retirement was inconceivable for the prospective conqueror of nature. But suppose, for the time being at least, he abandoned this role. Suppose he became a courtier, indistinguishable from Cecil or any other courtier. Suppose, finally, that through the regular course of promotions, he became one of the richest and most influential of officials in Her Majesty's service. Perhaps then, out of his own pocket, he could finance the great research enterprise, and so, sometime before his death, could come into his own again. As he had demonstrated, he was temperamentally "more fit to hold a book than to play a part." Moreover, his ineptitude in this past episode would be held against him. However, by the control of nature, or rather human nature, he believed that anybody could be a success in any profession. Using himself as a guinea pig, he now set about scientifically to prove this.

In the first place, he noted he had been much too plainspoken to qualify as a courtier. "He that is only real had need have exceeding great parts of virtue, as the (jewel) had need to be rich that is set without foil." Henceforth, he would be ceremonious in all his public appearances, "a little familiar with interiors," "keeping state with his equals," reserving his private thoughts for his disciples. In the second place, too often and too loudly, he had extolled his own merits. Henceforth, whenever the situation demanded self-promotion, he would do it through some alter ego like Tobie Matthew. Also he would pay more attention to the timing of his appeals, for "a wise man will make more opportunities than he finds." "Light gains come thick, whereas great (ones) come but now and then."

Another innovation was "the art of dissimulation," that is, the art of lying. For the most part all that was required here was a mysterious and secretive manner. Only on rare and great occasions, he believed, would he have to resort to the "outright lie." Finally, he had alienated the court by his conversation, which was almost exclusively concerned with the conquest of nature. At Christmas time, 1594, he had begun a notebook, which he called a "Promus of Formularies." Here he recorded not only the current small talk, but also morning and evening salutations and a rich variety of compliments. For example: "Wishing you all the best and myself occasion to do you service." "I desire no secret news, but the truth of common news." "I wish you fit as I am unfit." Before appearing at court he would consult this notebook and memorize the most appropriate greetings and salutations for that day.

Even more important in his transformation was the toughening of his "knee timber" by which he could better withstand the "pitching and tossing" of court life. During his ill-fated bid for office, he had begun a life-long drug habit. In the mornings he took three grains of nitre (natural sodium carbonate) in thin warm broth. This was to settle his stomach, and for the same purpose, once weekly, he took a "maceration of rhubarb infused into a draught of white wine and beer mingled." At bedtime he generally took a strong draft of March-beer to "lay his waking fancy asleep." But now on reflection, he decided that his troubles were psychological, not physical. And since the science of psychology (the "Georgics of the Mind," he called it) was still in its infancy, he pioneered it for his own guidance.

His imperial pretensions were still sound enough, he believed, but obviously they had blinded him to the political realities of his position. "We ought to be creatures of today," he concluded, "not of tomorrow, for tomorrow will have its turn and become today." It is enough if "we take thought for the present." Also he had been too worrisome, dwelling on his cares "longer than is necessary for just deliberation." Henceforth, he would face the future with the utmost realism: he would base his actions, not on "light, frothy, unequal, wandering dreams," but on "understanding and judgment." As to his moodiness, ultimately he would be like Diogenes, who could "check the sallies of the soul on the steepest precipice and make it, like a well-broken horse, stop and turn at the shortest warning."

It would be many years before he could prove his boast that a scientifically trained courtier was better than a natural one and "could beat him at his own bow." Moreover, he always had such difficulty in suppressing his "frothy" dreams, it was a wonder he ever proved it at all. But in this case, he transformed himself from inventor to courtier very quickly. By October 1595, when the Solicitor General's place fell at last to his rival (as he had anticipated) he was already in complete command of himself.

First, he apologized to Cecil and the others whom he had affronted in his outburst. Generously he assured them he had never doubted their loyalty. Then, in a long letter to Essex he coldly weighed what he had gained and what he had lost in his 2 ½ years' suit. "I have lost some [reputation], some time, and some means," he said. "But then for [reputation], it is a blast that goeth and cometh. For time, it is true that it goeth and cometh, but yet I have learned that it may be redeemed. For that (last) point of estate and means, I partly lean to the ancient opinion 'that a philosopher may be rich if he wills it.'" His uncle, he noted, had been a little too sympathetic, telling him that his failure was "more than a philosopher morally can digest." Bacon stoutly denied this. "Without any such high conceit," he said, "I esteem it like the pulling out of an aching tooth, which I remember when I was a child and had little philosophy, I was glad of when it was done."

Thereafter, doors swung open that had hitherto been locked against him. The Queen designated him "Counsel Extraordinary to Her Majesty." It was a unique position, "without patent or fee," depending wholly on her whim. Yet at the same time his "extraordinary access to the throne would be restored, and he would be consulted in some of her most important litigation. Moreover, since "the Queen was constant in her favors and made an end where she began," he had good reason to believe that when the next vacancy occurred among the high offices, he was "next the door."

Following the Queen's example, the ladies who had barely tolerated him accepted him as a full-fledged member of court society. Indeed, wherever he looked in "the very face of this court," he found "some addition of reputation." Modest as this success was, Bacon was delighted with it. If nothing else, he had proved his capacity to control nature in himself. Some day, no doubt, he would also prove his capacity to control nature in general, and each small triumph at court (it seemed) brought that day so much closer. When the Queen "saluted" him as she went to Chapel, Bacon proudly told his brother Anthony, "I doubt not but God hath an operation in it that will not suffer good endeavors to perish."

CHAPTER TWO

IN LEAGUE WITH ESSEX

"The genius of a single man can no more equal learning
than a private purse hold way with the exchequer."
—*Francis Bacon*

The rules by which the young Bacon had transformed himself into a courtier were sound enough. During this transformation, he had jotted them down in two different sets of notebooks and in two separate styles. In the first set, the style was concise and "highly spiced," more or less after the fashion of Seneca's epistles, but actually in a relatively new style called *Essays*. In the second set, the style was formal and scientific. The *Essays* were popular from the start. He permitted them to be copied and passed from hand to hand until 1597. When unscrupulous publishers then threatened to "steal unripe fruit from his orchard," he formally authorized their publication. Thus, a landmark was established in English letters, Montaigne having pioneered this style in France 17 years before.

His second set of notes was later incorporated in his philosophical work, *The Advancement of Learning,* and thereby established him as a pioneer in the science of success, such as it is. "It may seem a new and odd kind of thing to teach men how to make their fortunes," he wrote apologetically. "But for some men, success is harder to attain than virtue." Since then, Bacon's rules have proved helpful to some 13 generations of ambitious men—courtiers in the old days, businessmen and politicians in the new.[5] No doubt Bacon also would have profited by them, had he practiced them more regularly. But hardly had he put his foot in the door by this method, than he found another possible means to success—a means which he considered not so safe, perhaps, but certainly nobler and more in keeping with his dignity as the potential conqueror of nature.

In this role he called himself a "physician of state," or, as we would put it, a technical expert on government. By his intercourse with nature, he not only believed that he could "invent all things possible," and convert failures into successes, but that he could correct all social evils and establish a perfect monarchy or "a new ordering in man's troubled life and business." By a minute examination of the "causes of [social] ills, the constitutions of patients [states], the dangers of accidents" and, by accurate prediction of the future, he said, he could arrive at "the true method of cure." He did not claim infallibility for his remedies, but the next best thing. My method "affords more remedies than it breeds diseases." If one remedy miscarries, then another will resolve the "perplexity," and still another will serve "to carry things in suspense without prejudice." In this conviction, he offered himself to the Queen as a councillor superior to Burghley, Cecil, or any other courtier who relied on a few "receipts," rather than on the "true method of cure."

What can we say about Bacon's new system of government? Some of the remedies that he now proposed to Queen Elizabeth, such as the reform of the laws, have been adopted in the centuries since his death; others might safely be adopted many centuries hence. However, in recommending these remedies in his own time, he was obviously pushing his government too far and too fast. Bacon was well aware of this objection. Yet if only the Queen would give him the opportunity, he was certain that, by the "evidence of truth and gentle persuasion," he could establish a "just and lawful rule over men's understandings" and so transform his perfect monarchy from a dream into a working reality. This, of course, was a delusion comparable to his other delusion that given certain conditions, he could invent "all things possible." Even today, no nation, whether monarchy or democracy, has ever been so impressed with one man's "evidence of truth" that it would (for very

---

5   The actual number of generations is approximately 15 in consideration of today's date.

long, at any rate) dispense with its regular councillors in favor of that man. Yet it was on this delusion that his fantastic career was largely based, and here, too, he would ultimately destroy himself for the benefit of his disciples.

✺

The first man to encourage Bacon in his new role was the Queen's dashing favorite, the Earl of Essex. A handsome, supple youth with a red beard, he had come to court in 1586, and as a courtier later described his debut, "sure it is, that he no sooner appeared in court, but he took with the Queen and the courtiers." Thereafter he was almost constantly in the Queen's company. He led her palfrey in the triumphal procession on the night of the Armada victory in 1588. They rode together in the royal coach through the parks and woods around London, and they played cards together "till birds sing in the morning."

There has been much speculation about how far their friendship went. Bacon assured us that at 60 the Queen was far beyond the natural age for such "vanities," and that while she allowed "amorous admiration, she prohibited desire." However that may be, this 21-year-old Earl was a very gifted youngster in many ways, and was eager for a more responsible role in the government than this purely ornamental one. He was not only a patron of such poets as Spenser, but was himself "accounted as one of the best poets among the nobility," and he spent long hours of "bookish contemplations" in his country estate at Wanstead. Not only did he cut a fine figure in the tilt yard, but he was also a soldier of almost unbelievable courage as he had proved in two campaigns—one in Portugal without the Queen's consent and the other in Normandy, with her consent. Yet so helter-skelter were his gifts, so "rash and temerarious" was his temper, that the Queen would give him no position of responsibility. It was in the effort to prove his capacity for such posts that in 1591, he sought the advice of the potential conqueror of nature.

In reply, Bacon gave the Earl a positive plan of action. In this time of perennial crisis with Spain, the way to advancement, he suggested, was by organizing an efficient intelligence service. This advice was sound enough. There was no central intelligence agency in the Queen's court, and every privy councillor had his private staff of informants, "newswriters," and messengers or "Mercuries" posted in strategic places both at home and abroad. Burghley's staff was by far the best. But Bacon was sure he could organize an even better one for the Earl. Bacon was very contemptuous of the loose, almost poetic, standards that prevailed among the English informants. There was too much reliance on rumor, too much wishful thinking, too little regard for the facts. As he later told Essex, "To make a judgment upon [one bit of evidence] were like a foolish mountebank," making a urine analysis on "one water." The informants of Spain, he might have noted, were almost equally at fault in this respect. It was largely on the basis of an overly optimistic report of the pro-Spanish sentiment in England that the ill-fated Spanish Armada was conceived and executed. However, by scientific discipline, Bacon told Essex, the efficiency of an intelligence service could be vastly improved.

Essex agreed to Bacon's proposal; in his turn Bacon concluded that the Earl was the "fittest instrument for doing good to the state." Thereafter, Bacon tells us, "I applied myself to him in a manner which I think happeneth rarely among men. For I did not only labor carefully and industriously in that he set me about. But neglecting the Queen's service, mine own fortune, and in a sort my vocation, I did nothing else."

Bacon's first act, apparently, was to appoint his brother Anthony as chief secretary of the new intelligence office. Anthony had just returned from the continent, where he had had many years' experience as an informer for Walsingham, the former Secretary of State. Also, according to the biographer Aubrey, he was really "much beyond his brother Francis for the [practical] politics." As the service expanded, four assistant secretaries were brought in to help. Meanwhile, with Anthony's help, Francis gathered a rather impressive field staff with agents in Scotland, France, Holland, Italy, Spain and Bohemia, not to mention counter-spies in England. As to Francis' own role, he would be the "interpretor" or evaluator, through whom the incoming intelligence would be forwarded to Essex with recommendations, and by whom most of the outgoing instructions would be drafted.

In their early days together, because of his inexperience, Essex may have left his intelligence agency largely in the hands of the Bacons. But in its second or third year when they began tapping the correspondence of certain Portuguese refugees, his interest was piqued to such a high point that he turned the organization topsy-turvy.

From contemporary documents, we get a vivid picture of this. One morning in January 1594, Anthony, who lived as well as worked in Essex House, was summoned to the Earl's chamber. The Earl was being dressed by his servants. But even at this early hour, in the midst of a complicated toilet, he was totally engrossed in the intelligence reports. "He gave his legs, arms and breast to his ordinary servants to button and dress him, his head and face to his barber, his eyes to his letters." At Anthony's entrance, he suddenly tore loose from his servants, and with excited gestures informed Anthony of his latest discovery.

It is a "most dangerous and desperate treason" he said, worse than any yet reported by any of the overseas informants. The Queen must be informed at once, he went on. The whole plot must be made "clear as the noonday" and brother Francis must draft the report. A message was sent to Gray's Inn to bring him posthaste to Essex House. The messenger returned, saying that Bacon was out. So Essex dashed off the following note to be left at Gray's Inn for him: "Excuse my ill-writing. I write in haste and have my chamber full of company that break my head with ill talking . . . I will now draw some notes of mine own which I will reform and enlarge by yours."

By modern efficiency standards—or rather by Bacon's own standards, which were even higher than ours—this operation left much to be desired. In their most sensational revelation, for example, it now appears that their supposed villain, Dr. Lopez, was an English counter-spy in the employ of Walsingham, and not a spy for the Spanish King, though it was on the latter charge that he was tried, convicted and executed. Nonetheless, Bacon had made good his boast: he had provided Essex with the best intelligence service then available. By the end of 1596, all "matters of intelligence" were reported to be "wholly in the Earl's hands." Also, in the spring, Essex had been confirmed as a member of the Privy Council. As to the long-range influence of Bacon's agency, some scholars have seen here the origin of our modern objective press. For when newspapers first came into existence in 1618, which was in Bacon's own lifetime, they were generally undertaken as a side activity by the informants of privy councillors, and as we have seen, Bacon had set a new standard for this profession.

At any rate, it was in gratitude for this service that Essex had championed Bacon in his ill-fated suit, first, for Attorney General, then, for

Solicitor General. In the Queen's presence, Essex had several times offered to "sacrifice" his whole position as her favorite for Bacon's promotion. Riding in a coach with Sir Robert Cecil, he had bluntly told the latter how "strange" it was "that you don't advance your cousin." And he had told a high official that Bacon's advancement was not merely a personal matter, "but a public cause wherein your Lordship shall have honor to the world." So extravagantly did he sing Bacon's praises that Bacon's mother said, he had "spoiled all by his violent courses," though as we have seen, Bacon had already spoiled his own case by the extravagance of his own self-praise. Failing in this, Essex sought other means of repaying his benefactor. One day shortly after Bacon's final defeat, he appeared humbly at Gray's Inn and said: "Master Bacon, the Queen hath denied me yon place for you and hath placed another. I know you are the least part of your own matter. But you fare ill because you have chosen me for your mean and dependence. You have spent your time and thoughts in my matters. I die if I do not somewhat towards your fortune. [Therefore], you shall not deny to accept a piece of land which I shall bestow upon you."

At first Bacon refused the gift, saying that the Earl could not afford it. He reminded Essex of the Duke of Guise, who was once known as the greatest usurer in France, "because he had turned all his estate into obligations, and had left himself nothing." "Now, my Lord, I would not have you imitate his course." Essex insisted. And Bacon, having already sunk so much of his own wealth in his research enterprise and regarding himself as kind of a public institution, could not long resist. "If I grow to be a rich man [that is to say, if he could someday make profitable inventions], you will give me leave [I hope] to give it back to some of your unrewarded followers." At the same time, he reminded Essex that in his capacity as "physician of state," his first loyalty was to the Queen and that despite this gift, "I can be no more yours than I was." He described their relationship as a feudal one. But reading between the lines, it was clear that his chief interest in Essex was as an "instrument" for getting the perfect monarchy adopted by the Queen. So long as the Earl conducted himself in accordance with principles of this new government, the Earl could count on his loyalty as before. Otherwise, he could not. Later, when Bacon told Essex that "your fortune comprehendeth mine," this is precisely what he meant.

It should be obvious, at once, that Bacon's terms were impossible. Why, indeed, should the Earl continue indefinitely as the instrument for Bacon's great schemes? By Bacon's new system of intelligence, it is true, he had prospered. But the next item on Bacon's political agenda, the reform of the laws, was completely unworkable at this time. Moreover, at bottom, the Earl was not temperamentally equipped for this role, nor, indeed, was any other courtier. During their early days together, Essex had tried to fit himself as a perfect councillor in Bacon's perfect monarchy. He had even given Bacon a special license to "speak plainly" to him whenever he failed of the mark.

Sometimes when Bacon took this license too literally, the Earl would swear at him and banish him from his presence, but the next day would be full of apologies. "I cannot be other than your friend," he would say, "either upon humor or mine own election."

After a few years of this, Anthony told his brother that the Earl is getting over his "rawishness" and "clean forsaking all his youthful tricks." But this was wishful thinking. For the higher the Earl rose at court the more he became his tempestuous self. After two years in the Privy Council, he threw over the traces altogether. Instead of reforming the laws or creating an "inward peace" for the country, as Bacon wanted him to do, the Earl devoted himself to the organization and command of a land-sea expedition against Spain.

In this enterprise, the Queen indulged her favorite, a contemporary wrote, like an "overuberous nurse with a suckling child."

In June 1596, he was at Plymouth, in joint command with Lord Henry Howard of an expedition against Cadiz, the Spanish naval base from which a second Armada might be launched. Meanwhile, using his special license for plain speaking, Bacon had tried to talk Essex out of it. "My Lord," he said on a similar occasion later, "when I came first unto you, I took you for a physician that desired to cure the diseases of the state. But now I doubt you will be like those [quack] physicians which can be content to keep their patients low because they will always be in request." "Essex took this plainness very well," Bacon reported, "as he had an excellent ear and was most patient of the truth." But "in the very entrance of a great action," he was so supremely self-confident, that he flung the quackery charge right back in Bacon's face.

"The case of the realm requires an expedition at this time." Besides,

Essex went on, if he had followed Bacon's timorous counsel, he would never have attained half his present "greatness." "Look you, sir, how I have won the Queen, and now tell me whose principles be true."

Bacon shook his head in despair. "My Lord, these courses be like to hot waters. They will help at a pang, but if you use them [continuously], you shall make them stronger and stronger [and] you shall spoil the stomach."

It was characteristic of Bacon that he could always see the folly of others with uncanny accuracy, but could never see his own folly in trying to save them from theirs. In the debate over the Cadiz expedition, Bacon, as usual, was wrong in the short run and right in the long run. His short run error was due, in part no doubt, to his chagrin at losing the Earl as an instrument for his perfect monarchy. But his correct predictions of long-term doom was based on his observation that Essex was not equipped for his new role and that whatever Essex might think to the contrary, he was really better off in the old one. Perhaps Bacon recalled that during the ill-fated Normandy campaign in 1591, Essex had displayed more courage than sense. He had trailed a pike like an ordinary foot soldier, and gone "a-hawking" in a district swarming with the enemy, and lost 3,000 out of 4,500 troops in ill-considered sorties of one kind or another.

Surely, some such fiasco as this was in the making, and with far more serious consequences. With his ambition unsatisfied, Essex would become a danger to the state. The Queen, hitherto so indulgent, would be forced to put some mark of her displeasure on him; Essex would retaliate by an act of disloyalty. "Ambition is like a choler," Bacon wrote later, no doubt from his experience with Essex—"a choler which is an humour that maketh men active, earnest, full of alacrity and stirring if it be not stopped. But if it be stopped, and cannot have its way, it becometh adust, and thereby malign and venomous."

On the strength of this uncanny prophecy, Bacon might have washed his hands of the Earl and sought some "new instrument" for his schemes. Better yet, he might have abandoned these schemes altogether and by regular service, subsidized his research college. Had he taken either of these two courses, he would have stood on firm moral ground, for all obligations between the two men had been discharged. However, any such sensible action as this would have been inconceivable for this "would-be conqueror of nature."

In the first place, rightly or wrongly, he felt that but for him, Essex would never have got himself into his present predicament. In the second place, though it was clearly the Queen's responsibility to get Essex safe out of it again, in her present infatuation she obviously could not do this. Hence, inevitably the responsibility would fall on him. For a time now, it looked as if Essex was indeed deserting his friend. But the truth was that he was merely manoeuvering for a new position at court—a position of strength in which he could act as a balance of power between the rival Essex and Cecil factions and "keep things steady," at least, until Essex should come to his senses again.

How quixotic a gesture this was hardly needs further comment. Only a year or so before, he had resolved henceforth to base all his actions on facts rather than on "light, frothy, wandering dreams." Also he had written: "Mean men, in their rising, must adhere. [Only] great men that have strength in themselves [can] mantain themselves indifferent and neutral." As Counsel Extraordinary to the Queen, he was technically a "mean man." But once again, his extraordinary (though not infallible) foresight had blinded him to the realities of his scheme, for the perfect monarchy had already been accepted; the Queen had already lifted him to a great place at court, and among other things had entrusted the Essex problem exclusively to him. Had this dream been a reality, no doubt all his actions would have been reasonable enough. Nobody could have charged him then with being a meddler. On the contrary, he might have saved Essex for a long and useful life in the reorganized Queen's service. Yet as matters stood, however well intended his subsequent actions may have been, they were presumptuous in the extreme and, rightfully, he would be punished for them.

�֎

It was not till after Essex's return from the Cadiz expedition that Bacon assumed his new role as a disinterested neutral. But even before the expedition, his complicated plan must have been fully matured in his mind, for it was executed flawlessly. First, by very conceivable means, he informed the public that he had made a clean break with the Earl. When he spoke with the Earl, it was at Gray's Inn, or "somewhere else than at Court." When the Earl embarked on subsequent expeditions, Bacon would excuse himself from the embarkation ceremonies, saying that "ceremonies are things infinitely inferior to my love and to my zeal."

Finally, he carried on a public flirtation with the Earl's enemies, and formerly his own—the Cecils, father and son. "Your Lordship is [now] a principal owner of that mite (I cannot call it talent) that God hath given me," he told his Uncle Burghley. Meanwhile, through his brother Anthony, who had remained loyally in the Essex camp, he kept the door open for a resumption of their former relationship. It was in this strange posture, incidentally, that he dedicated the first slim edition of his immortal *Essays* to Essex. On January 30, 1597, Bacon dedicated this work (it included but 10 essays, while the final edition had 37) to his "loving and beloved brother" Anthony; a week later, on February 8, Anthony "transferred his interest" to the Earl.

Contrary to Bacon's expectation, as every schoolboy now knows, the Cadiz expedition was a great success. Indeed, it has gone down as one of the most brilliant day's work in military history. 26 years later, Bacon would describe it enthusiastically as follows: "This journey was like lightning. For in the space of 14 hours, the King of Spain's Navy was destroyed and the town of Cadiz taken. The town was a fair, strong, wellbuilt and rich city. … It was manned with 4,000 soldiers on foot and 400 horses. It was sacked and burned, though great clemency was used towards the inhabitants." But at this time Bacon was not so much exultant as relieved that Essex had got away with it. "I am infinitely glad of this last journey, now it is past," he told the Earl. Nor was Bacon humbled in the slightest that his tragic forebodings had proved so misguided. On the contrary, he was now more concerned about Essex than before, fearing that his success would make him all the more headstrong. Nonetheless, Bacon went ahead with his plan anyway. Assuming his role as a disinterested neutral, in effect, he now tried to frighten Essex into a more realistic view of himself.

Essex was the hero of the hour—a hero more popular with the London mobs even than the Queen. All the great spirits of the age paid tribute to him and urged him to greater triumphs. A preacher at St. Paul's hailed him as another Caesar or Alexander. Even Lord Henry Howard, his fellow commander, did him honor, assuring Lord Burghley that "there is not a braver man in the world than the Earl is, and I protest, in my poor judgment, a great soldier [too]." But according to Bacon, all these people were mistaken and Essex was now in great personal danger.

"A man of nature not to be ruled, of an estate not grounded to his greatness, of [enormous] popular reputation. I ask whether there can be a more dangerous image than this represented [by your enemies] to a monarch of her majesty's apprehensions?" If this was the case, then obviously Essex had no alternative but to renounce his glamorous career and return to his more humble role as a social reformer. Instead of seeking a new military office such as Master of the Ordinance, Essex should seek a purely political one, Lord Privy Seal, for—"a fine honor, quiet place, and worth £1,000 a year." Instead of parading with his troops before cheering throngs, he should champion unpopular but essential legislation. Such renunciation, Bacon admitted, was psychologically difficult and would demand the utmost in self-discipline. If Essex could not bring himself to it, he should elevate and honor some rival military hero, like Lord Mountjoy, who might share his laurels with him.

History records few, if any cases, of such renunciation as Bacon proposed to Essex. Nor did any of Bacon's dark prophecies have the slightest effect on the glamorous Earl at this time. However, during the next year or so, events played into Bacon's hands.

The following spring, Essex, in joint command with Sir Walter Raleigh, embarked a second expedition, which was intended to intercept and capture a Spanish treasure fleet off the Azores. Here again, his losses were slight. But by a series of miscalculations, he had let the treasure fleet slip past him and, in October 1597, returned home more or less empty-handed. Essex refused to admit defeat. By his "violent courses" he tried to force the Queen to give him command of yet another expedition in which he might redeem his honor. This time the Queen did not indulge her favorite. But in February 1598, when Sir Robert Cecil, who had been "fully stalled" as Secretary of State following his father's death, went off to Paris on a diplomatic mission, she appointed Essex to serve temporarily in his place.

Now that Essex willy nilly had fallen back into a purely political office, Bacon abandoned his neutrality and once more offered his services to him. Essex had been piqued by Bacon's strange manoeuvers. "As it is the manner of men seldom to communicate when they think their courses are not approved," for at least four months Essex had broken off all relations with him. But in his new post, the Earl obviously needed Bacon, and soon the two men were amiably arguing points of high policy as though nothing had ever come between them.

It was Bacon's hope that once the Earl had become preoccupied with some great problem, a problem that "hath been much neglected" and by the peaceful solution of which "your Lordship will purchase much honor," his military ambition would be forgotten. Such a problem, in short, would serve for what we call occupational therapy, and such a problem was currently before the Privy Council, namely, that of Ireland. After all, no conquering army could cope with a nation like the Irish, he told Essex. Essex should try to "cure the root of the disease" by a thorough reformation of abuses, extortions, and injustices. For the Irish were such an enemy as the ancient Gauls or Germans or Britons, "who too placed" their felicity only in liberty and the sharpness of their sword. The Romans, "who had such discipline to govern their soldiers, and who could levy them from the whole world, ever found they had their hands full of them." However, on the one hand, the Irish problem would not wait for Bacon's elaborate program of "reformation." On the other hand, as one courtier said, the Earl was still as much "transported with an overdesire after that deceitful fame of popularity" as ever. In March 1599, against his better judgment, the Earl found himself at the head of another expedition, this time with orders to suppress an Irish rebellion.

When this expedition embarked on the Irish Sea, the soothsayers were unanimous in their auguries of a triumphal return, and the great poets who had always been so enamoured of the Earl, once more paid tribute to him. "We're now the general of our gracious empress, as in good time he may, from Ireland coming," wrote Shakespeare probably on this occasion, "how many would the peaceful city quit to welcome him!"

But once again, Bacon did not share the general optimism. On the contrary, "I did as plainly see his overthrow, chained as it were by destiny to that journey, as it is possible for a man to ground a judgment upon future contingents." In short, despite all his well-meaning efforts, he had failed to save his friend from his tragic destiny. Yet now on the eve of battle, he managed, in part, to conceal his pessimism; he, too, gave the Earl some encouraging words. On the basis of oracles "none superstitious and yet not all natural," that is to say, on historical principles, he told Essex that since he was fighting in the cause of civilization against barbarism, he was bound to win out in the end. At the same time, he reminded Essex of an old saying "that things go ill, not by accident, but by error." To emphasize this, he then enumerated the shortcomings that had caused the Earl so much grief in the past—his blind courage, his headlong strategy, and above all, his insubordination to the Queen. If worse came to worst, he said, you must remember that in such a great cause as this, the honor of participation exceeds the disgrace of failure.

Despite his failure to save Essex, Bacon had won the respect of the Queen by his prophecies and his good intentions. Throughout the Irish campaign, she consulted him about it probably more than any other councillor. For hardly had Essex landed with his troops in Ireland than she began to find fault with her favorite. Instead of attacking his enemy, the Earl of Tyrone, in his northern stronghold, Essex spent his time in more or less useless actions, liberating petty strongholds in central Ireland and listening to the cheers of their grateful defenders. "I am giving him £1,000 a day to make progresses with," the Queen complained.

But why do you permit this farce to continue? Bacon asked. "If my Lord were brought home with some suitable diversion, such as the Treasury, he might [yet] be a useful ornament in your court." But "to discontent him, and yet to put arms and power into his hands may be too strong a temptation for him." Elizabeth may, indeed, have been strongly tempted by Bacon's counsel, but before she could make up her mind about it, Essex brought himself home. He had won nothing but a worthless treaty. Without permission he had left his army in the field. Now, with only a small personal escort, he swept dramatically into the palace, pushed past the palace guards into the Queen's bedchamber, and there, fell at the Queen's feet, crying out that he was the victor.

At this point, even more than before, Bacon should have abandoned his efforts to save the Earl. For one thing, though the Queen was consulting him in this matter, she had made no commitment to follow his advice. In the second place, by his previous efforts he had not only failed to save the Earl, but had suffered serious reverses in his own fortunes. Simply to provide for his everyday needs, he had sold the property that Essex had given him in 1595.

As to his creditors, he had recently been arrested for a small debt of £300, on which he had defaulted. If not for a friendly sheriff who arrived and "recommended" him to a "handsome" detention house in Coleman Street he would have spent the night in prison. Yet nothing could make him abandon this futile quest. So far as he could see, the Queen herself was still unable to cope with the situation. So, he now gave her detailed instructions on just how Essex should be handled.

Before Essex could be restored as the Queen's favorite, according to Bacon, Elizabeth would first have to acknowledge the failure of his Irish expedition. This was a delicate operation. The Earl should be given a public, or semi-public, trial in which he could defend his actions and in which it would be shown that "my Lord was not wounded on his back." After the trial, he should be "restored to his former attendance, with some addition of honor to take away discontent."

Instead of that, the Queen acted on impulse. On the day of his return, she had Essex arrested and confined in York House under the care of the Lord Keeper. One month later, through the Star Chamber, it was declared simply that his conduct of the Irish campaign had been unsatisfactory and that the Queen was displeased with him. The declaration, as Bacon had foreseen, proved abortive. None of the Earl's recent failures had discouraged his followers in the slightest; for this last one, they blamed not Essex, but the Queen. The white walls of the palace were covered with abusive scrawls against her. Pamphlets were secretly published and circulated, some of them clearly seditious, urging Essex to punish the Queen by seizing the throne from her. Four months later, the uproar was so great that she was forced to adopt the Bacon plan. She would give the Earl a chance to defend himself at a semi-public hearing in York House. But she did not like to admit that, in this instance, Bacon's judgment was better than hers. Just to remind him of his fallibility, she ordered him to join the rest of her Learned Counsel at the abovementioned hearing.

Bacon objected to this on two counts. In the first place, if he was to continue his usefulness in the case, it was essential that he preserve his detachment from both sides. In the second place, the part assigned to him in the prosecution he regarded as ridiculous. Sir John Hayward had dedicated his *Life and Reign of Henry IV* to the Earl, saying that "with your name adorning the front of our Henry, go forth to the public happier and safer."

But in popularizing the usurper, Henry IV, the Queen thought that Essex and the author were conspiring to prepare the country for the Earl's own usurpation. "Madam," Bacon had said, "the fault of the author is not treason, but felony. For he hath taken most of the sentences of Tacitus [the Roman historian], translated them into English and put them into his own text." As for Essex, surely patronage of learning was the least of his vices. "I should reckon it for one of her highest favors if her Majesty would have me forbourne in this business," he told his friends. Yet the Queen would not release him. At the hearing, according to his own report, he was more precise than the other lawyers in stating the nature of the Earl's offense. And if he also spoke more sharply than they, it was due "partly to the superior duty I did owe to the Queen's fame," and "partly to his intention" to conceal from the public his continued loyalty to the Earl.

On the latter point, there can be no doubt of his success. For when the judgment of the court was rendered, when the Earl had been suspended from all his offices, and thereby had "his wings clipped," the fury of the Essex supporters was diverted largely from the Queen to this "busy" Bacon. Bacon's life was threatened, his name libelled. Yet he still had no reason to regret his part in the case. And now that the unpleasant preliminaries were over, he dedicated himself to the pleasant finale—namely, to the reconciliation between the Queen and her former favorite. One day soon after this, the Queen asked him about his brother Anthony's latest cure for the gout. Bacon replied that at first he seemed to be getting better, then worse. The Queen then berated all physicians who prescribe one method of cure and "have not the discretion to change their medicine."

"Good lord, Madam," said Bacon, "how wisely and aptly you speak of medicine ministered to the body and not consider that there is the like occasion of medicine ministered to the mind." With this in his preface, Bacon then launched into his main theme. The Queen had many times declared that she wanted to reform Essex, not ruin him. But now that she had punished him, now that she had drawn all the "ill humors" out of him, it was time, he said, that she "administer strength and comfort to him." "Your present courses, however, are fitter to corrupt that to correct any [ambitious] mind."

Having thus firmly planted the idea of a reconciliation in the Queen's mind, Bacon then approached the Earl proposing that he, Bacon, ghostwrite the latter's correspondence with the Queen so that the reconciliation might more quickly be consummated. By the sentence of the court, Essex would continue under house arrest "until it should please her Majesty to release him." As yet, the Queen had not seen fit to do this and it was in his "cage" at York House that Bacon made his remarkable proposal to him. Essex was doubtful at first of Bacon's good intentions. "I can neither expound nor censure your late actions," he said, being ignorant of all of them save one. But when Bacon had given him a full and honest account of these actions, he willingly consented to the plan. Several letters were now written on this basis—dictated by Bacon and dispatched in Essex's handwriting.

But one day it occurred to Bacon that there was a flaw in this scheme; it was out of character for Essex to bare his soul to the Queen as Bacon was having him do, and that sooner or later, the Queen would find them out. To remedy this defect, he devised a new scheme even more remarkable than the other. This time, he ghostwrote what purported to be an exchange of letters between Essex and his brother Anthony. These letters were brought before the Queen's eye by accident as it were. Therin Essex described himself as a broken man whose only hope was to be restored to the Queen's good graces. While through Anthony, Elizabeth was pictured as a grieving lady whose actions had been forced on her "merely from necessity and point of hone" and whose love for Essex, her former favorite, could easily be rekindled.

Meanwhile, through frequent visits to the Queen, Bacon watched the Queen's reaction to his cure and was gratified to learn of its momentary success. After each letter the Queen expressed her amazement and her delight at the change in the Earl's attitude towards her. After a month, she permitted him to return to Essex House. Two weeks later, he was given full liberty. At any moment now, Bacon reported to Essex, he could expect to be restored to her presence chamber. But now, unfortunately, with Bacon no longer at his side to restrain him and to ghostwrite his letters, Essex reverted once more to his "violent courses." The monopoly of sweet wines which was his chief source of income would lapse within a few months. Unless the Queen would guarantee its renewal, Essex wrote with characteristic bluntness, she could no longer count on his love and submissiveness. Bacon tried to explain away this blunder by telling the Queen that all men are moved by two desires—the one for perfection, and the other, for self-preservation. "Perfect" as Essex now was in his love and devotion to her Majesty, he was certainly as much entitled to his "stake" or "prop" as any courtier. But Elizabeth was proud. She would not accept a love so basely alloyed. She not only broke off her correspondence with the Earl, but also with Bacon.

Having lost his second and final battle with destiny, Bacon was now prepared to take his punishment. What Essex's next move would be, he didn't know. For Essex had also slammed the door on him, and likewise, on his brother Anthony, who had hitherto kept him informed of the Earl's doings. Yet he feared the worst. On New Year's Day, 1601, he advised the Queen of how things stood with him. "A great many love me not because they think I have been against my Lord of Essex. You love me not because you think I have been for him." However, he was consoled by the thought that he had played the game "without respect of cautions to myself" and in good faith with you both. Now, "if I do break my neck, I shall do it in a manner as Master Dorrington [a famous suicide] did it [who] walked on the battlements of the church many days, and took a view and survey where he should fall." A month later, his prophecy was fulfilled. On February 8, Essex with three hundred of his ardent followers marched on London, shouting that the Queen had sold the country to Spain—apparently in an effort to raise an army for a further march on the palace. But at this critical hour, his London supporters abandoned him. So he marched back to Essex House, where the Queen's forces overwhelmed him, and took him prisoner.

When Bacon heard of the uprising he said only that he was relieved that it had passed off so quietly and inefficiently. If "some base or cruel persons" had attempted this action, he told the Queen, "it might have caused much blood and combustion." But Essex and his friends, being amateurs, "knew not how to play the malefactors." Yet when he considered what a truly prodigious effort he had made to prevent this very thing, he became very angry. Instead of blaming himself for misjudging the subject of a benevolent, but ill-considered action, he blamed the subject. Later he would regard the Earl more compassionately, and in all future references to the Earl's uprising, he would speak of it as "a fatal impatience" or "an attempt at revolt and rebellion" rather than "treason." But now he did not mince words. On February 11, when the Queen asked him to join Learned Counsel in taking depositions in the case, he made no protest. Again, on February 19, when the trial opened in Westminster Hall, he was patently more anxious for the Earl's conviction than anyone else.

At one point in the trial, Essex attempted to use Bacon's action on his behalf to discredit Bacon. The Earl had argued that his uprising was nothing more than a counter-move to check a much more serious uprising by Sir Robert Cecil and his other enemies at court. Bacon denied this. "There are no such enemies, no such dangers," he said, looking the Earl in the face. "All whatsoever you have or can say in answer hereof are but shadows. And therefore, methinks, it were best for you to confess, not to justify."

Calmly Essex then rose in rebuttal: "To answer Mr. Bacon's speech, I say this much and call forth Mr. Bacon against Mr. Bacon." He revealed how Bacon had written certain letters for him, in one of which he had explicitly said that Essex's enemies were actively working against his restoration to favor. Had he chosen to do so, Bacon could easily have explained this apparent discrepancy. But there had been enough digressions in the trial already, and he did not choose to make any more.

In reply, he said only that he had "spent more time in vain in studying how to make the Earl a good servant to the Queen and to the state than I have done anything else. Those letters, if they were here, would not blush to be seen for anything contained in them." Yet the Earl's point was a telling one. For until he explained the rationale of his strange behavior in a pamphlet two years later, very few of his contemporaries believed that he had been anything but a troublemaker in this business.

Thus Bacon's second campaign for high office under Queen Elizabeth came to its inevitable end, and in his more rational moments, he would admit that for a second time, his dreams had blinded him to the realities of his position. "My mind has been on other things," he told a friend, "and in absence are many errors." Had he withheld his benefactions until the Queen had fully authorized them, then, no doubt, his council would have been effective. In this belief, 11 years later, in his essay *Of Ambition*, he passed along to posterity much the same counsel that he had vainly given to Elizabeth and Essex. This, of course, was his legitimate role—as a general counsellor for the world, and not for his own time.

Meanwhile, his private world had fallen into complete ruin. In 1603, he wrote that he had entered politics partly for patriotic reasons, "because a man's own country has some special claims upon him more than mankind at large," and partly because, if successful, "I should have a large command of industry and ability to help me in my [research]." Now, he said, "my zeal [has been] mistaken for ambition;" at 42, "my progress [has been] too slow," and since "I was by no means discharging the primary duty that lay upon me," namely, to conquer nature, "I put all those [other] thoughts aside, and in pursuance of my old determination, betook myself wholly to this work." However, with neither men nor resources at his disposal, by his own statement, he could not have gotten very far with this enterprise. Moreover, again by his statement, if a new and more friendly King had not ascended the throne at this time, his enterprise might have been stillborn.

CHAPTER THREE

SHAMING THE PROFESSORS

"Why should a few favorite authors stand up like Hercules'
columns to bar further sailing and discovery?"
—*The Advancement of Learning*

On March 24, 1603, after a brilliant 44 years' reign, Queen Elizabeth died. A few days later, by arrangement with Sir Robert Cecil, King James VI of Scotland crossed the Tweed River to take throne as King James I of England. Bacon was delighted, if not openly exultant. Elizabeth had failed to adopt his enterprise and the social reorganization that went with it, he believed, because she was "rather a sojourner than an inhabitant of the present world," interested only in short term considerations. But here was a King like himself, with a highly speculative mind—a King who "had not merely drunk at the true fountain of learning, but who had a fountain of learning in himself."

Four years earlier, James had expounded the principles of what he called "kingcraft," in a book, *The Basilikon Doron*. Unusually candid and excellently written, it was "one of the soundest, [most scientific] and most profitable works" Bacon had ever read, and had filled all England with "a good perfume or incense before the King's coming." Also, James had made a name for himself as a patron of the arts and sciences. Many years before, he had visited the astronomer Tycho Brahe in the observatory that the King of Denmark had built on the island of Hven. James had been so impressed with Brahe's work that he had written a poem about it. Here, in short, was the perfect patron for his own enterprise, and while James set the troubled affairs of England in order, Bacon might have all the men and resources he needed for the orderly conquest of nature. "I was born for his Majesty's service," he told his friends enthusiastically. And this, indeed, proved to be true, though not quite in the way that Bacon expected.

At first, Bacon thought it would be easier to deal with James on the political front than on the scientific. On this assumption, at any rate, he sent him samples of his new techniques. At intervals, he sent him a rough draft of royal "Proclamation" for immediate use, and a dissertation on the political lessons to be learned from nature. In all reforms, he wrote "nature and time must be left to do the work" for "artificial forcing will only spoil the operation"an excellent bit of advice that Bacon would often urge on others, but almost always ignore himself. Receiving no acknowledgement on these works, he then requested a personal interview with the new King. This was difficult.

The King had been a strong Essex man. Essex supporters would be favored in the new regime (it was already understood that James would pardon all those who had taken part in the uprising), and Essex's enemies, save for Robert Cecil, would fall. Momentarily, Bacon swallowed his pride and made a peace offering to Southampton, the leader of the Essex faction, saying, "I may safely be now that which I was truly before," which, as we have seen, was partially true. Southampton, unfortunately for Bacon, did not reciprocate the offer. But Bacon's brother, Anthony, who had died, perhaps of grief, a few months after the Earl's execution, had also made connections in the Scottish court. And it was largely through these connections that Bacon was granted his interview.

When Bacon met the royal party somewhere north of London, the King was at loose ends. A thousand Scottish beggars had followed him down from the border, and half of London, it seemed, had come up to meet him. Wherever he stopped for the night (and every provincial nobleman and bishop vied for the privilege of putting him up), he was beset with courtiers, seeking new positions or confirmation of old ones. An awkward, bashful man, he complained that his English subjects were treating him like a six-legged calf or some other monstrosity.

By the time Bacon had joined the temporary court, he had decided to make no official changes for "a year and a day," or at least until he had met with Sir Robert Cecil, on whose stooped shoulders most of the responsibility would fall. "I have had no private conference to any purpose with the King," Bacon told the Earl of Northumberland. "No more hath almost any other English." Bacon, in turn, was neither wholly taken with James nor wholly repelled. "Your lordship [he went on] shall find a prince the farthest from the appearance of vainglory that may be and rather like a prince of the ancient form than of the latter time. His speech is swift and cursory, and in the full dialect of his country. He affecteth popularity by gracing such [fashions] as he hath heard to be popular, and not by any fashions of his own." In their conversation together, "his Majesty rather asked counsel of the time past than of the time to come," so Bacon had had no opportunity to explain to the other the enormous implications of his suit.

Back in London, Cecil (now Baron Cecil of Essendine) placed still another obstacle between Bacon and the new King. Cecil's reasons for this may be readily understood. In the pre-Coronation turmoil, Cecil was making heavy weather of it, and with Bacon at his side, trying to change the rules of government, his task would not be any easier. James "spends £100,000 yearly on his house which was wont to be but £50,000," Cecil later complained to another suitor. James had created one thousand new knights, pensioned numerous Scottish earls, and was constantly falling off his horse "which is no more than may befall any other great and extreme rider at least once every month." When someone congratulated Cecil that he did not have to kneel before James as he had before Elizabeth, he replied, "I wish to God I still spoke on my knees." Thus, when Bacon asked his cousin what his chances were under the new regime, Cecil told him with complete candor that he would be better off out of it than in it. Bacon might still consider himself "Counsel Extraordinary" as before. But if he would stay away from the palace, Cecil would make it worth his while. As a pledge of his good faith, he offered Baon a short-term loan of £300 to help him pay off a pressing debt.

Bacon accepted the bait without cavil, and when Cecil made good on his offer, he said that he was glad their long misunderstanding had come to an end. "To be plain with your Lordship, that will quicken me which slackened me before. For then I thought you might have more use of me than now I suppose you are likely to have." Bacon did not deceive himself as to the real reason for his cousin's opposition: it was his old "impediment," his ambition to be recognized on his own terms as conqueror of nature. However, under the new King (he thought), instead of an impediment, this ambition would be an asset.

On the political front, Cecil, Southampton, and the other courtiers might seal him off from James with an iron ring. But on the scientific front, no power on earth could prevent their joining hands in a great and fruitful collaboration. "My ambition now," he told Cecil, "I shall only put upon my pen—upon a book to be called *The Advancement of Learning*." This book, he told Cecil after the completion of a similar volume later, "may appear vulgar to vulgar minds, but it may be that the deeper (and wiser) intellect [of King James] will not be left aground by it, but rather (as I hope) be carried along." At the very least, the book would maintain Bacon's "merit" with "the times succeeding."

The character of this book was dictated in large part by the King's great interest in academic matters. At every opportunity, on every "progress" through the countryside, not excepting his pre-Coronation march to London, the King would detour to pay a visit to Oxford or Cambridge. These visits were invariably attended with great ceremony. The faculty, dressed in their scarlet gowns and mortarboards, would present him with honorary degrees; the students would shout "Vivat Rex" and sometimes perform plays or masques for him.

But James also regarded himself as a scholar equal or better than his hosts. "Should not a King be the best clerk (writer) in his own country and does not wit best become royalty?" he would ask them. Then stripping off his robes of office, he would vie with professors at their own profession. Sometimes he debated points of logic and theology with the students. Sometimes he sat as a member *ex officio* of examining committees for the higher degrees. He even gave lectures, based on his published works. Whatever he did, he always enjoyed himself immensely, and when the time came for him to resume his official burdens, it was always with difficulty that the Queen and the royal party tore him away. On one such occasion, after a visit to the new Bodleian Library at Oxford where the books were chained to the shelves with iron links, he remarked: "Were I not King, I would be a University man. And if it were so that I must be a prisoner, I would have no other prison than this library and be chained together with these good authors."

Now it had occurred to Bacon that if the King loved learning to this extent and believed in the "merit of those who labor for its propagation," he would naturally give an attentive ear to any proposal such as Bacon's enterprise, calculated rapidly to speed up its "propagation and development." Under the existing administration, the Universities did almost no research worthy of the name. About a century before, they had gone to great lengths to revive the old stock of Greco-Roman learning. But they were so overawed by the majesty and authority of the ancient sages that they felt relieved of any responsibility to improve on them. These sages had brought knowledge to absolute perfection, one professor said; it was foolhardy, if not blasphemous, for anybody to tamper with this knowledge.

By the same token, they also felt it unnecessary to concern themselves with the great, burgeoning, Elizabethan world in which they lived—either with its unprecedented voyages of discoveries, or its towering achievements in letters and politics. To be sure, Bacon wrote, there are so many worthy men in the faculties of learning, men of "subtle and strong capacities" and "with an abundance of leisure." "But their minds are shut up in a few authors as their bodies in the cells of their Universities which keeps them ignorant both of the history of nature and of their times." No wonder then that their books are "so laborious and so empty"—"cobwebs of learning, admirable, indeed, for the fineness of the thread, but of no substance or profit."

By contrast, how productive and how useful learning could become, if the facilities of the Universities were turned over to him. For fear of unduly alarming the King, perhaps, he refrained from promising "the discovery of all causes" and "the invention of all things possible at this time." But he did urge the King to undertake a "well-purged" inventory of all natural phenomena and of all "monsters, vegetable, animal and mineral" which he considered the main prerequisite of this achievement. Also, out of his foreknowledge of the future, he drew up a list of about 56 works or inventions, some of which might conceivably be forthcoming prior to the inventory.

Among these projects not already mentioned were: a scheme for progressive education ("the doctrine of schoollearning" with "the suiting of studies to a man's genius"); a new international scientific language ("a philosophical grammar"), made up of Latin conjugations and tenses and the best French, Italian, and English figures of speech, forming "one perfect pattern of speech"; propaganda analysis ("a collection of sophisms with their confutations"); finding "short and commodious methods of calculation in business"; new painkillers ("the laudable means of procuring easy deaths"); biography ("the lives of all eminent persons"); and scientific astrology, showing the real, instead of the fancied, effects of stars on men.

For those inventions that fell within what we call the social sciences, new chairs perhaps would have to be founded with his own disciples installed in them. But otherwise there need be no delay. At a given signal from him, teams of investigators, composed both of students and professors, would leave their "monastic cells" and dig deep under the surface of contemporary English life. At vacation times, the professors would shuttle back and forth on horseback to professional meetings to discuss their tentative findings. For just as "the anointment of God establishes a brotherhood in Kings and Bishops, in like manner there should spring up a fraternity in learning and illumination." Finally, when agreement had been reached about the findings, they should be published in book form. Nor should the professors be discouraged by the multitude of books already on the shelves. For these were full of errors, and bad old books could be destroyed by good new ones, "as the serpent of Moses was said to destroy the serpents of the enchanters."

In the field of political science ("state policy"), for their own safety, he would urge the faculty to go slow, for "civil government is [still] supported by authority and not by demonstration." However, he did suggest that under Lord Chancellor Egerton, a research project be started "for one just and complete history" of the two Kingdoms of England and Scotland—and he urged that as many documents, sayings, and letters as possible, excluding state secrets, should be turned over to the historians. All other departments should "resound as in mines with new work and advances."

On the other hand, for inventions in the natural sciences, that is for the conquest of nature, not only would new chairs have to be founded but the whole enterprise would have to be started "anew," discarding all the rubbish of the ancients and proceeding by a secret method that he would later reveal to them. At present, he admitted, most people think the natural sciences are "idle" and "futile," forgetting that it is "on the proficiency of this branch of learning that the state of every other branch depends." When rich men died, they left foundations for law and or for medicine.

Indeed, at Cambridge, a country gentleman had recently founded a lectureship on witchcraft. But as yet, no chairs had been founded for geology, astronomy, or chemistry, nor, for that matter, for history, modern languages and literature, or "civil policy." Therefore, let "munificent patronage" be granted in these new departments, with high salaries to attract "the ablest scholars," and with all the necessary equipment. Let the astronomers, for example, be abundantly supplied with "spheres, globes, astrolabes, maps, and the like." Let the chemists not be lacking in "engines" or "furnaces." Let the medical researchers have all the cadavers they wanted.

Under existing law, they were permitted only six bodies of executed convicts a year; the dissections were conducted with great ceremony before students over a three day period with morning and afternoon sessions and banquets between; and no research was attempted. If this law could not be changed because of religious prejudice, then the practice of animal vivisection should be encouraged. As another aid to medical research, physicians should be encouraged to revive the old Greek practice of making and keeping clinical notes on their patients.

This plan was well within the King's prerogative, Bacon pointed out. Through the Vice Chancellors of the Universities, who were also members of his Privy Council, "a thorough reformation could be made of such [studies] as are ill-suited to the age." Just what his own part in the reorganization should be, he did not make clear. Later he told Cecil that "I shall content myself to awake better spirits like a bellringer which first up to call others to Church." Nor can anyone doubt that he would have been content with this role, if he could get no better one.

However, he had also pointed out that "soundness of direction" and "conjunction of labors" were as essential to its success as royal patronage. Since he alone had the know-how for this (or so he believed), he must have assumed that if the plan were adopted, he would be its chief administrator, either with some office at Trinity or St. John's College in Cambridge, or at Magdalen College in Oxford (where presumably, he already had some disciples). Or, perhaps some high and hitherto unknown office would be created for him—an office in which he would be called the "Interpretor of Nature," or in modern terms, an Office of Research and Development.

It was possible, though not probable, that the speculative King would adopt Bacon's bold plan. But even if he had, clearly the professors would not yield their stronghold without a terrific struggle. In those days, it must be recalled, the Universities were not primarily creative institutions, but rather shrines dedicated to the preservation of accepted truth. It was the professors' duty not to discover new knowledge, but to protect and preserve the old from all unsettling influences. Thus it was no accident, as Bacon said, that "no fit men [he should have said, "so few fit men"] have been engaged to forward those sciences which yet remain in an unfinished state." For it was inconceivable to the professors that there was anything worth knowing that the Greeks and Romans did not know.

The Baconian dream of "man's empire over nature" was preposterous to them. Sixty years later, when Bacon's disciples finally broke the professors' monopoly of the learned world by organizing the Royal Society, the professors would do everything they could to disrupt this enterprise. They would steal the dogs and goats out of the Society's medical laboratories. They would ridicule the great ladies and gentlemen who came with their servants to look at the moon through a telescope and at fleas through a microscope. They would charge the inventors of a "waywizer," or a mileometer for a coach, with subverting the "happiness of this generation and the next." Yet, how much more bitterly would they oppose the Bacon plan, which in effect, called for their complete abdication?

From previous encounters with the University officials, Bacon knew precisely what he was up against. However, he would make no concessions to them. If they called him down for arrogance, he would "answer simply that modesty and civil respect are fit for civil matters; in science nothing is to be respected by truth." Indeed, in his imagination, he had already been installed as the chief administrator of the new program, and from this vantage ground, he gave them a drubbing that they would never forget.

Briefly but pointedly, he surveys the intellectual globe of his times, "noticing what parts lie wasted and uncultivated, abandoned by the industry of man," and indicating roughly how these deficiencies could be remedies under his administration. "Many of these deficiencies will be much censured," he went on—"some as being already complete, and others as too difficult to be effected." Yet, in the long run, no inventions and no discovery would be beyond the powers of such a college as he had outlined for them. Even if its execution required "a succession of ages," rather than in "the hour glass of one man's life" (which of course was his private hope), he would still consider the enterprise as of the utmost importance. However, if the hostility proved too great, if the professors should succeed in blocking his plan, he could still carry on, he suggested with the few dissident professors who were already secretly engaged in this work, and the few private persons outside of the Universities who might support it sufficiently.

�֎

Take the old science of astronomy, he suggested. From the Greek Ptolemy, the professors had inherited a universe, "noble, perfect and incorruptible"— a universe in which each heavenly body had "his own repair and crystal house." The earth was at its center. Around the earth, the sun, the moon, and the planets "are wheeled around in perfect circles with eccentrics and epicycles to preserve their circular motions." In the outermost layer, 1022 stars were fixed like nails in the vaulted roof of a hall.

For almost 2000 years, this astronomy had served to explain the facts. But in recent years, under the intense scrutiny of trans-Atlantic sailors, the heavens had begun to act strangely. Planets were found wandering loose from their "crystal houses"; new stars flared up, one of them so brightly that it could be seen in broad daylight; comets went zooming across the skies. Indeed, between 1572 and 1604, there had been at least 10 incidents in the heavens that the old astronomy could not adequately account for. The professors were in a dilemma. Obviously something was wrong either with their astronomy or with nature, and unwilling to abandon their astronomy, they blamed nature. Solemnly, they now announced that the world was coming to an end. "God has not intended to give men eternal possession of the Earth," one of them declared, "nor permanence to the universe, otherwise he would not have permitted such discord in the heavens above nor on the earth below." John Norden, a cartographer, added in rhyme:

> "All the creatures that he made so fast
> Shall by degree, alter, wear and wast."

It is difficult to imagine the gloom that was spread by such announcements as this, supported as they were by so much authority. Even the atomic gloom of our times probably does not equal it.[6] Now and everywhere, men anxiously peered at the heavens, looking for some cosmic incident that would touch off the final collapse, and there must have been thousands of false alarms. According to Ashley, at every comet the country plowman predicted "a great flood in the midst of his furrows," the "silly shepherd" dreamt of flying dragons, and "he lighteth no sooner on a quagmire but he thinketh this is the foretold earthquake, whereof his boy hath the ballad."

From his intimate "conversation with nature," Bacon had no difficulty in seeing that such gloom prophecies "ought all to be despised, and ought to serve but for winter talk by the fireside." What the professors needed, he declared, was some new system of astronomy, "giving the substance, motions and influences of the heavenly bodies as they really are" to replace the old system, which was clearly obsolete. Oddly enough, a few enterprising professors had already pioneered this new astronomy.

Half a century before, Copernicus, a Polish mathematician and churchman, had suggested that the old astronomy could be abandoned for a new one under which the earth revolved around the sun instead of vice versa. This system was not perfect, he admitted, but was more in accord with the facts and, if it proved to be correct, then natural explanations could be made of other "strange disturbances." So revolutionary was this system that the professors paid very little attention to it; in *The Advancement of Learning*, even Bacon dismissed it very hastily. However, five years later, in 1610, Galileo, an Italian mathematician, turned a telescope on the planet Jupiter, and there in its system of satellites found visual proof that Copernicus was right.

This "strange piece of news" caused a tremendous stir. Kings and princes, bishops and archbishops in every country of Christendom clamored to have a look at "the four new planets rolling about the sphere of Jupiter." Bacon was delighted at this fulfillment, or partial fulfillment, of one of his important prophecies. "This is a most noble discovery," he wrote, "so far as credit can safely be given to demonstrations of this nature."

However, Galileo had by no means exhausted the subject, he cautioned.

---

6   The gloom of our current global climate crisis would be another contemporary example to use here.

No conclusions should be made as to the Copernican system until the telescope had been applied to other objects "equally worthy of consideration." The professors, on the other hand, refused to look through the telescope at all. "There are 7 windows of the head—2 nostrils, 2 eyes, 2 ears and a mouth. There are 7 days of the week, and 7 metals. From this and many other similarities in nature, we gather that the number of planets is necessarily 7." Therefore, this professor concluded, the new planets reported by Galileo must be optical illusions.

But even in those days, there were limits to public credulity. Unable to support their authority by argument, the academic authorities of northern Italy attempted to do it by force, referring Galileo to the Dominicans and the Jesuits for prosecution on religious grounds. Another deficient department of learning was medicine; here the textbooks were more than 1400 years old and obviously unsuited to the times. True, the physicians were highly organized. In 1518, the Royal College of Physicians had been founded to distinguish the university-trained physicians from "common artificers"—smiths, weavers and women—who were then "taking upon them great cures."

Yet, almost a century later, the distinction was still hard to maintain. The cures then in vogue, such as bloodletting for the "sanguine," laxatives for the "choleric," scorpions, coxcombs, spider webs, and woodlice for others in quantities depending on the relative position of the Sun and the signs of the Zodiac—these cures were often worse than the disease. Seventy years later, when accurate statistics finally became available, it was found that at least one out of every eight patients who were admitted to the London hospitals never came out alive. In 1600 the hospital mortality rate was probably twice as high. It is not difficult, then, to account for Bodley's remark to Bacon that not one in a hundred followed the prescriptions of their physicians. Like the clergy, Bacon added, the physicians had only power "to bind and loose," that is, to constipate and to purge their patients.

At this time, moreover, the prestige of the medical profession was on the wane rather than on the rise. The "coming-in" of King James had coincided with the "coming-in" of another great plague. Within the first year of his reign, London would lose 43,000 persons, or about one-sixth of her population, chiefly from this cause, and the licensed physicians simply could not cope with the situation. The plague, they said, was caused by putrefying flesh and the foul airs emanating therefrom.

At their suggestion, ordinances were written and promulgated to "sequester" the infected parties. The houses of infected parties were marked with huge red crosses; none were permitted to enter them save the physicians themselves. For protection against infection, the doctors advised chewing orange peels or angelica root, smoking tobacco, or stuffing the noses with rue and henna. Thomas Dekker, the playwright, has described an antiseptic coach of the time. It was "a fearful pitiful thing," he said, "all hung with rue from the top to the toe of the boot to keep the leather and nails from infection: the very nostrils of the coach horses were stopped with rue."

Yet despite all these ingenious precautions, nothing could stop the infection. And when the physicians also began to suffer casualties, they joined the city officials in flight, turning their posts over to the various quacks and witch doctors who were always ready to work their magic cures "to the high displeasure of God, great infamy of the faculty [the Royal College of Physicians] and the grievous, hurt, damage and destruction of the King's liege people."

It was during the worst of this plague that the Coronation took place in Westminster Abbey. Attended by 16 earls, 10 bishops, the Lord Mayor of London and a few others, it was a private, almost a secret ceremony. The crowds that had come to London to do the King honor had returned home. "The solemn entry and passage through our City of London and all other festivities," he had told them, "would be held over" till the following winter, when, inevitably, the plague would run its course. Two days before, at Cecil's invitation, Bacon appeared in Whitehall to be knighted. "I wish that the manner might grace me, since the matter will not; I mean that I might not be merely gregarious in a troop," he had told his cousin imperiously. Yet with three hundred other gentlemen knighted at the same time, and with church bells tolling the dead in the deserted city outside, this ceremony was no more auspicious for him than the Coronation for the King.

If only the physicians had been provided with "specific cures for specific diseases" based on a truly scientific pathology, Bacon noted later. Nor did he doubt that under his administration, the Royal College of Physicians, could produce such cures. (Actually, it was not until the 1860s that Pasteur brought forth the first of them.) At any rate, whether Bacon could or couldn't, there was no excuse for the professors' statement that the plague was incurable. This declaration, he wrote, was nothing but a shield for "negligence and carelessness" and a confession of "ignorance." By clinging to their outmoded textbooks, they have "delivered men over to death as unjustly and with more abandon than ever did the Roman tyrants."

❈

Perhaps, the most interesting feature of *The Advancement of Learning* was the language in which it was written. This was scientific English, or at least, an attempt at it. (If he had had time, he would also have devised the new international scientific language that he had mentioned in his agenda.) The emphasis in the new English, naturally enough, was on clarity. Don't puff up your arguments with eloquence, with "finely flourished" phrases, and other "luxuriances" of style. Don't define everything and confute everything. Above all, don't affect an omniscience or a "completeness" that you don't have. Report your findings as concisely as possible, and let them be "so stated as to carry with them an invitation to others for adding and lending their assistance."

Prior to the publication of the *Advancement* he had asked two friends, Bishop Andrewes and Tobie Matthew, to act as his literary "Inquisitors"— to read the manuscript and make sure that he had observed his own rules. "Make some little note in writing where you think (to speak like a critic) that I do perhaps fall asleep, or where I indulge in wit, or where in fine I give any manner of disadvantage to myself." All criticisms of this kind were taken into account in the final draft. As to criticisms of matter, "my judgment is fixed, and not accessible by any man's judgment that goeth not my way. Yet even in those things, the admonition of a friend may make me express myself diversely" he said.

Having invented this new language, Bacon then proceeded to criticize the style then in vogue among the professors. The professors, he noted, did not lack literary talent. On the contrary, "there be many good (word) painters for hand and color" among them. The trouble was that their talent ran to charming poetry or narrative prose-poems, which are the delights of "the most ignorant ages and of the most barbarous peoples," but which would be no use whatsoever in scientific research. At this very moment, 40 professors,

20 from each great University, were engaged in a great 7 year literary enterprise—the English translation of the Holy Scriptures. This work, which was completed in 1611, and which has become known as the King James version, was so magnificent that posterity is inclined to forgive its authors their bitter-end opposition to the research movement.

But in 1608, when Bacon looked about for some professor to translate the *Advancement* into Latin "without manifest loss of sense and matter," some professor who could write Latin with the same clarity that he tried to achieve in English, he couldn't find one. The only volunteer was Dr. Playfere, Professor of Divinity at Cambridge. But as Archbishop Tenison, another disciple, said 50 years later, Playfere was so flustered by his mission that he "strained, cracked and disabled" his natural genius.

Oddly enough, even Bacon did not succeed altogether in writing scientific English either. This was because, at bottom, he was just as much of a poet as the professors; no matter how suggestive his inventions might be of our own, at this time and place they were still as beautiful and insubstantial as the professors' "crystal houses." Bacon admitted these poetic digressions, and was rather apologetic about them. "It is impossible to expound new ideas," he said, "without the aid of similes and metaphors." "Besides," he added, "a touch of elocution," though it interferes with the "severe inquiry of truth," adds to the "force of practical writing."

Yet despite these digressions, it is truly amazing in point of verbiage and grammar, how closely Bacon's language resembles the modern scientific English that he was striking at. Certainly, he came closer to it than any of his contemporaries. During the next century, his disciples would again take up this project. Some of them would write as well as preach scientific English, thus serving as obscure links between Bacon and Swift, Addison and Fielding—the great prose masters of the 18th century.

✄

Over the centuries, *The Advancement of Learning* would prove to be one of the most stimulating and influential books ever written. But now, the University officials found it so shocking that they would not dignify it with a formal rejoinder: their doors were shut tight against both Bacon and his enterprise. His friend, Sir Thomas Bodley, the founder of the Bodleian Library mentioned above, was his chief informant among the University men. After a long interval and after much amiable prodding from Bacon himself ("you are, I bear you witness, slothful, and you help me nothing"), Bodley finally made his report: "You deserve happiness and honor, the fit reward to the full of your dessert. But unfortunately, you have fallen into the study of such a study as is not worthy such a student." The fact was, Bodley went on, that you "could not impanel a substantial jury in either University that would acquit you of error."

Had Bodley been drafted for this jury, he too, would have voted against the would-be conqueror of nature, for "like a carrier horse, I cannot bank the beaten way." However, Bacon's real error, which concerned his administrative powers rather than the plan itself, escaped them. "If we scrap the old sciences," Bodley went on naively, "and begin anew, we should instantly return to barbarism. A thousand years hence, we should have less theoretical furniture than we have now." From other sources Bacon found that this was the majority view. The provost of King's College, Cambridge sarcastically told one of Bacon's men that after reading the *Advancement*, "he found himself in a case to begin all his studies anew, since he had lost all the time of his studying before." A famous Oxford scholar was quoted as having said, "A fool could not have written it, and a wise man would not."

With the professors so unanimously against him, it was almost a foregone conclusion that the King would be too. "Like the peace of God," James later remarked, the books of Sir Francis Bacon "surpasseth all understanding."

Bacon was disappointed, but his faith in his enterprise was undiminished. "There is no worse augury in [such] matters than that derived from unanimity. One should immediately examine what error or fault he has committed when the multitude concurs with him." Moreover, if the professors and the King didn't recognize its merits, many other people did—some secretly inside the Universities and some outside—and they organized little research colleges of their own. One such college was established secretly in the Tower of London right under the King's nose.

Its facilities consisted of an assaying furnace for "proving metals" and a little hen house in the garden that had been converted into a still. Its staff included Dr. Harriott, a mathematician who had owned and operated a telescope before Galileo, and Sampson, a chemist. Its patron was the short-lived Prince of Wales, Prince Henry, acting without his father's knowledge. Its leading spirit was the famous Sir Walter Raleigh, who had been implicated in a conspiracy against the Crown, and who now occupied himself with scientific research to pass the time away.

Nothing much would come out of this little college save a highly inaccurate *History of the World*, written, Raleigh declared, according to the rules of that "excellent learned gentleman, Sir Francis Bacon." Also, Raleigh invented a Great Cordial, which was supposed to cure people of a variety of ailments, but which sometimes killed them. Yet if Bacon could organize these people into one great research federation to be financed, perhaps, by the sympathetic Archbishop of Canterbury, then (he thought) he could carry on his work just as effectively as by outright control of the Universities.

Unfortunately the times were just as unfavorable for research federations as for research colleges in the Universities. Also from this point of view, he had published *The Advancement of Learning* at the worst possible time, his publication date October 1605, coinciding with the Gunpowder Plot, which marked the onset of a great wave of religious hysteria. Bacon may have known that he was working against an unfavorable deadline. He began the book in the spring of 1603 just after James' accession.

It was exhilarating work. "I have now for a time enjoyed myself," he told Bodley. "My labors, if I may so term them, are the comfort of my other labors." After the first year, he had completed but one slim volume "which I account but as a page to the second book." From March to December, 1604, he was occupied in Parliament and during the next six months, he raced through the second book, the main portion, so quickly that he said he could not do justice to it.

Of the five first copies of the *Advancement*, the first Bacon gave with great ceremony to the Earl of Northampton, "the learnedest councillor in this Kingdom" for transmission to the King. The other four went to Egerton, the Lord Chancellor, who was to have supervised the history-writing project, Cecil (now Lord Salisbury) and Lord Buckhorst, the Vice Chancellors respectively of Cambridge and Oxford, and Sir Thomas Bodley. But nobody paid much attention to the book, for at much the same time a large cache of gunpowder, 36 barrels in all, was found in the cellars under the House of Lords. Also, standing or crouched near-by, an arsonist was found, fully equipped with fuses and tinderbox. When this man was brought before the King (his name, Guy Fawkes, has become infamous in English tradition), he confessed freely that he had been hired by a group of Catholic fanatics "to blow the royal family back to Scotland," and Parliament with them.

Further investigation revealed that Fawkes was telling the truth. Seven of his confederates were rounded up, several others were killed in a brief skirmish with the Sheriff of Hewell Grange; in a sensational public trial the plotters were tried and executed. Yet this was by no means the end of the incident. In his charge to the jury, Sir Edward Coke, then Attorney General, had said: "Such people are retrograde of nature and unworthy to tread the earth." They should be drawn, hanged, quartered, then "their remains should be set up in some high and eminent place to the view and detestation of men." This, apparently, was the temper of the country, and under the King's direction a great crusade was launched to ferret out concealed Catholics wherever they might be hid.

In a series of public letters, the King undertook to shame the Pope for his alleged part in the plot and to try him before a jury of his peers, the Kings of Europe. Parliament wrote new restrictive laws, turning Catholics in effect into second class citizens, forbidden to travel or to practice any dignified profession. Even the universities took part in the crusade: among other things, an oath of allegiance was administered both to faculty members and students alike. There was nothing remarkable about this, for, as we have seen, the Universities were then creatures of the government and responsive to government policy. However, many professors, we may imagine, embraced this anti-Catholic crusade because it gave them a pretext for publicly ignoring Bacon if not for silencing him altogether.

One night, Bacon was interrupted in Gray's Inn, his provisional headquarters, by a delegation of the principals and ancients "of Staple Inn, all solemn and impressive in their varicolored gowns." A fellow named Beard, they said, had been overheard in a tavern in dangerous and seditious talk. "The Gunpowder Plot was a brave plot," he had said, "and I, for one, regret that it has failed." This information had been passed from a gentleman's servant to the gentleman himself and thence to the authorities of Staple Inn. The latter had formally examined Beard and decided that he must be a "Papist or [Catholic] practiser."

The dispassionate Bacon was not so sure. "These," he said, "be bad words, but general." However, thinking it "not good to neglect anything at such a time," he agreed to report the incident to Salisbury. This episode occurred about four days after the discovery of the Plot. But its meaning in terms of his hopes for a research organization of one kind or another was already plain to him. From the strictly rational point of view, he could see no reason why science and religion should conflict: the two enterprises were separate and distinct. Yet he also knew that "in every age a blind and immoderate zeal for religion has been a troublesome and difficult opponent for science." In the present instance his own orthodoxy was not in question. But Tobie Matthew, his chief assistant at Gray's Inn and incidentally, his chief assistant-to-be in his proposed research college, was highly suspect.

At the moment, Matthew was out of the country. About May 1605, he had left for a grand tour of the continent and so had missed all the exciting events narrated above. When he returned, however, in the spring of 1607, he revealed that in the course of his travels he had become converted to Catholicism. This announcement created a tremendous stir. Matthew's father was the Bishop of Durham, one of the pillars of the established church, and a bitter opponent of "that most damnable and heretical doctrine of the Church of Rome."

Hence it became a matter of high public policy to bring young Matthew back into the fold, or at least, to get him to take the oath of allegiance. Great pressure was brought against him to this end. The Archbishop of Canterbury kept him in protective custody for many months, but without success. The King personally lectured and catechized him, but again without success. Finally he was sent to prison with hints that worse would follow. "So light a punishment will make him rather more proud and perverse," said Salisbury.

Bacon was as shocked as anybody else at the apostasy of his alter ego. In no uncertain terms he told him of his abhorrence of it. "And I entreat you much, sometimes to meditate upon the extreme effects of Catholicism in this last Powder Treason; fit to be tabled and pictured in the chambers of meditation as another hell above the ground." Yet at the same time he could not deny that Matthew had been "miserably abused" for his convictions. "Has the world grown to such an ecstasy as to reject truth in [learning] because the author dissenteth in religion?" "Are men so set to despise the means of their own good that they would destroy this enterprise which is for the betterment of their own bread and wine?"

Bacon refused to believe it. And though he was unable to take Matthew back in his provisional headquarters at Gray's Inn, he did apparently use his influence with Salisbury, getting him safely out of the country. Meanwhile, he paid frequent visits to Matthew in his cell, and provided him with manuscripts for editing and comment, and otherwise thrashed over the plans for his new college as though nothing had happened. Also, when Matthew was paroled prior to his exile, Bacon opened his lodgings to him as a refuge. Here, Bacon was anticipating the principle of toleration that would be so vital for the future research movement. And since toleration was so little understood by his contemporaries, he was made to suffer for it. One critic expressed his surprise that a man of his connections should "give so much countenance to one so affected."

"Nothing can be more dangerous," said another.

Many years later when Bacon's character was in question, Matthew testified, "It is not his [intellectual] greatness that I admire, but his virtue. It is not the favors that I have received from him (infinite though they be) that have thus enthralled and enchained my heart, but his whole life and character." Of more immediate interest, when Matthew was exiled to the continent, he reciprocated the favors Bacon had done him by acting as an overseas missionary for Bacon's proposed research federation.

Bacon had told him that he valued "your own reading of [my books] more than your publishing them to others." Yet since the enterprise was then temporarily stalemated in England, he obviously welcomed the idea of converting some "learned men beyond the seas." It was for this reason that Bacon had tried to have the *Advancement* translated into Latin, the universal language of the time. Unfortunately, the "learned men beyond the seas" were as much in the grip of religious hysteria as those in England, and there, Bacon's Protestant partisanship was as much of a handicap as Matthew's Catholic partisanship at home. Matthew did, indeed, make some converts to the idea. But in so doing he himself fell under suspicion. His letters became increasingly cryptic; the messenger who bore them, Bacon complained, "had travelled so long amongst the sadder nations" that Bacon couldn't make out what Matthew was up to.

By 1609, Bacon's organizing drive had come to a halt, and clearly would continue in abeyance until the world-wide religious hysteria subsided. He compared himself to "the miller of Huntington that was wont to pray for peace among the willows. For while the winds blew, the windmills wrought and the water mill was less customed"—the windmills being the anti-scientific Universities and the water mill, his proposed federation. Yet here again, God would not let "good endeavors" perish.

Despite all his unpopular and dangerous demonstrations on the scientific front, on the political front he was now making progress—as we shall see in more detail presently. So far he had risen no further than the Solicitor General's office. But if his luck held, he would soon be Attorney General, and then finally, Lord Chancellor, the highest office of the realm. Thus at last he could see an end to his difficulties. Under his direction, perhaps, the King would put an end to this disastrous religious hysteria. Also, perhaps, the King would force the Universities to swallow the research program that he had outlined for them in *The Advancement of Learning*.

Meanwhile, out of his own pocket (as he had formerly planned to do), he would establish a model college of his own. Perhaps he could not invent "all things possible" in this college. But at least, he could invent enough of them so that his disciples would carry on the enterprise after his death.

In the exciting years that followed, with all the heady distraction of high office, Bacon might easily have forgotten this difficult task. In 1609, he would publish *The Wisdom of the Ancients*. Here he would argue, perhaps with tongue in cheek, that the new discoveries "that he and his men were trying to draw out of [their] hiding places into the light" had already been known to a civilization more ancient than the Greeks; inadvertently they had been wrapped up "like a soft whisper" in Greek fables and parables. With this last appeal for public support, he fell silent, and would remain silent for 10 years thereafter.

Yet hardly a week passed that he did not add something to his college, either in fact or in the imagination; hardly a pound did he earn that he did not invest directly or indirectly in the enterprise. And he was constantly circulating manuscripts and arguing technical points with his allies and disciples, as in his debate with Galileo on the cause of the tides. Like a merchant, he kept a running ledger in which he "entered all manner of remembrance of matter, form, business, study" concerning his various activities. The "waste books" he kept current by throwing out obsolete pages and writing new ones to take their place.

During the vacation week of July 25–31, 1608, for example, he seems to have devoted himself almost exclusively to this activity, that is to say, to taking stock with himself of where he was going and where he had come from.

By careful examination of these notes, moreover, there can be no doubt that the conquest of nature was the great passion of his life and that his other enterprises were merely tributary to this one. At the proper moment, when his scientific work was in some "degree of forwardness," he would take the wraps off it, and show himself to the world once more in his favorite role as the potential or actual conqueror of nature.

CHAPTER FOUR

THE RACE WITH SALISBURY

"And certainly there is a great difference between a cunning man and a wise man."

—Bacon, Essays

Bacon's decision to return to this mission was made probably as early as the King's first meeting with Parliament on March 15, 1604. At that time, he was still bound by his informal agreement with Cecil "not to meddle in the King's affairs." However, in January, as in the previous election under Elizabeth, he had been returned to the Lower House from Ipswich and St. Albans.[7] Standing in the back of the hall with the other members, he saw the King blunder away the good will that he had enjoyed on his accession. Then in the weeks following, he saw the situation deteriorate into a deadlock between a liberty-loving Parliament and a tyrannical King.

Bacon was terribly shocked at this. If these "new fashions" were continued, he noted, there would be a popular uprising. (Actually, the uprising did not occur until 36 years later.) Yet, on the other hand, if the King would let him "found in this isle" "an apt seat" for civilizing "the rest of the world," then no doubt, this great tragedy could be avoided. On this assumption, he ignored his agreement with Cecil and thrust himself into the thick of the battle.

---

7   He was selected by both constituencies but decided to sit for Ipswich; his place at St. Albans went to Tobie Matthew.

In short order, he managed to get himself appointed to some 29 committees of the Lower House, including the important Committee on Grievances. Also he was mentioned for Speaker of the House against Sir Edward Phelips, the King's choice, and although not elected to this post, he would often be their spokesman in the palace where he "was extraordinarily entertained at dinner."

For the great purpose that was now uppermost in his mind, King James was by no means as hopeless in Bacon's eyes as in those of other men. At this very session, he had come forth with one of the most "memorable" and forward-looking measures Bacon had ever heard of. Holding the two crowns respectively of Scotland and England, it had occurred to him that the two countries should be united with all trade barriers knocked out and common citizenship established. "I am the husband," he had told the Commons, "and all this island is my lawful wife. . . . Therefore, before I die, let there be one worship of God, one kingdom entirely governed, one uniformity of law." Bacon had agreed with this. But he could not agree that the measure was so plausible that it should be adopted on the King's say-so alone, without preliminary discussion or debate, or as the King put it, "that it be embraced and be received by a hallelujah."

The King "hasteneth to a mixture of both kingdoms, faster perhaps than policy would conveniently bear" he noted. If James were ever to become a model King out of Bacon's book, he must not merely devise far-sighted measures, but also win support for them honestly and aboveboard.

Admittedly, this was not easy. The King and Bacon apart, there was hardly a public man in the Kingdom who approved the measure. A century would pass before it would again be seriously considered and partially enacted. As one member of Parliament put it, if this proposed Union of the two kingdoms is a marriage, it is certainly a disadvantageous one from the English point of view.

On the one hand was England, "with orchards swelling with fruit, pastures fat with kine, waters full of sails, a thriving people with inexhaustible fisheries, woods and mines." On the other hand was Scotland—"a land of crags and storms, without resources, peopled by a rude race without genius, and with no ships except a couple of rotten hoys." If the merger went through, both the English cloth manufacturers and the English merchants would suffer serious losses. So unfavorable did it appear that many patriots suspected that it was nothing more than a cynical device by which James could convert their rich motherland into a Scottish satellite. Unwittingly, James had encouraged this suspicion by pensioning some half dozen Scottish Earls and favorites out of his English budget.

Reluctantly, James was made to agree to a full Parliamentary debate on the measure in accordance with English custom. However, he asked that the members use their "liberty with modesty" and that proper respect be shown to the Crown. "I like form as much as matter," he told them. "It shows respect and I expect it, being a King as well born (suppose I say it) as any of my progenitors." Yet, in view of the tremendous antagonism aroused by the bill, such a decorous debate as this was out of the question. All the ancient wheezes against the Scots were now revived, and new ones, much more acid and bitter, coined.

In his play, *Eastward Ho!*, poet Ben Jonson suggested that instead of bringing the Scots into England, they should be sent to Virginia "for we should have ten times more comfort of them there than here." But now with his plan under attack, James had lost his sense of humor. He got the last laugh on Jonson by locking him in the Tower. The same high-handed treatment now became standard for the opposition faction in Parliament. Any member making quips at the expense of the Scots ran the risk of being summarily picked up and left to repent his irreverence in the Tower.

Meanwhile, Bacon had got himself appointed to a Royal Commission set up to draft the bill. He was "graced by the Commons with the first vote of all the Commissioners selected for that cause," and from the beginning, seems to have been its most active spirit. Here, inevitably, his power was limited. In view of the King's blunders, it must have been obvious to him very early that Parliament would never adopt this measure. However, by the excellence of his own performance, he attempted to show James how it might have been adopted, if only Bacon had been put in charge of it.

In the first place, instead of stifling criticism, Bacon encouraged it. Only he advised the opposition faction to look at the proposal, not from the point of view of their private or professional interests, but from that of the nation as a whole; he asked each of them, for the time being, to act like a King. A King, he told them, is not a merchant ("I do not single out this estate in disgrace, but only for an instance of a private profession"), a lawyer or a country gentleman. He must think and make decisions according to the "true and

worthy considerations of state." To the same end, Bacon had them adopt the
rule that no decision would be reached the same day it was proposed. They
must sleep on it overnight.

This Commission with its 48 members was an unwieldy body. Like the
Parliament from which it was largely drawn, it included men from many
professions and backgrounds, English as well as Scotch—2 privy councillors,
2 ambassadors, 4 lawyers, 2 ordinary citizens, 4 merchants, and 16 country
gentlemen. Yet, after only six weeks of deliberation, he brought them to
an agreement that was unanimous save for one lone dissenter, Sir Edward
Hoby, a radical.

When the bill came up for discussions on the floor of the Lower House,
Bacon then corrected the second of the King's errors. Instead of calling the
opposition disrespectful or disloyal, he answered all their arguments, no
matter how absurd. For it was another sound principle of debate that "no
prince should measure the danger of discontentments by this, whether they
be just or unjust." Who is this Scotchman that they were all so much afraid
of, he asked—this cheap bare-legged, red-cheeked beggar? He is a myth, a
phantom, and it was just as true to say that he was proud and haughty as to
say the opposite. The typical Scottish gentleman, doting on dress and show,
would rather starve at home than betray his poverty abroad.

In proof of this argument he pointed to the fact that though the King
had already lowered the bar on immigration, very few actual Scots had taken
advantage of it. Even if they had, what harm would it do? England had need
of immigrants to fill up her empty spaces. He did not mean London, which
was then seriously overcrowded. But in the wastelands (as he would continue to point out from time to time) there were cities to build, marshes to
drain, and textile factories to set "on going," while in the rivers and seas there
was an "Indian wealth," the hidden and rich "treasure of fishing."

But this was just the beginning. Falling back on his prophetic powers, "none superstitious and yet not all natural," he conjured up for them a
magnificent picture of what lay in store for them, if only they would adopt
this measure (and perhaps others he had in mind). A new nation would
arise out of the combined Kingdoms—a nation greater than Englishmen
had ever dreamed of before—a nation which Bacon named "Great Brit-
tany," or Great Britain.

"The seas are open, your merchants will embrace the whole compass of the world, east, west, north and south." Planters will follow the merchants in Ireland, in Virginia, and elsewhere so that in times to come, there will be "little sisters" to Great Britain wherever a man may look. At present, he admitted, England was still a second class power. But when all these potentialities were counted, "in forces truly esteemed" she is "one of the greatest monarchies that hath been in the world." "For certainly the kingdoms here on earth have a resemblance with the kingdom of heaven, which our Savior compareth not to any great kernel or nut, but to a very small grain, yet such a one as is apt to grow and spread."

"It is simply insufferable," he concluded, turning once more to the opposition, that Spain with a few American gold mines, should dream of great empire, while this island "with the best iron in the world [that is, the English yeomanry], should think of nothing but reckonings and audits, of mine and thine, and I cannot tell what."

Bacon's oratory had much improved since the days when he had stood breathlessly in Parliament, and taken his cues from his brother or his alter ego, Tobie Matthew. By his system of scientific memory-training, he had developed his memory to such a degree that he could now deliver a lengthy text with only a few notes to guide him. By a study of what he called "the colors of good and evil" (what we now call semantics) he had ready-made retorts for all opposition sharpshooters.

But in the present instance, there weren't any sharpshooters. In previous encounters he had flattened them and scared them off. One of them had rather have "his will than his wish," "another charteth too high a compass to shoot near." "I should willingly assent to your speech" he had told a third, "If we were not come hither for physic [medicine] than for music." As to his countenance, he had also mastered the science of facial control. In general, he believed that "speech and countenance should reinforce each other."

On this great occasion, he adopted a kind of dignified inscrutability so that with his purple robes and his rakish hat, he looked like "an apothecary's shop pot, painted on the outside with apes and owls and antiques, but containing within sovereign and precious remedies." Ben Jonson tells us that when Bacon made a speech, his audience could not get enough of him and "the fear of every man that heard him was lest he make an end." This time the combined weight of his manner and his matter must have been overpowering. We can imagine how he held them, "fearing to cough or look aside without loss" while he spoke, and how they crowded around him when he was finished.

✻

Despite his prophetic insight and his amazing oratory, Bacon could make no more progress with the Scottish Union plan than the King.[8] Moreover, all of Bacon's other remedies were doomed to failure for the same reason, namely, that they were anywhere from one hundred to five hundred years in advance of his times.[9] In his sober moments, Bacon was willing to face this fact. However, as has been said before, he believed that if only the King would raise him to high office (the higher the office the better), he could somehow close the gap between his remedies and the times. "For good thoughts, though God accept them, yet towards men are little better than dreams, except they be put into act. And that cannot be without power and place."

Later, he would regard King James as the chief stumbling block in this great design. But now, oddly enough, the King encouraged him in it. During the course of the Scottish Union debate, the King had told him that he was a peace-loving King who valued the servants who brought him "victories of peace" (or near victories) as much as warlike Kings valued the generals who brought them "victories of war." As early as August 1604, James had confirmed Bacon as a full-fledged member of Learned Counsel, a life pension of £60 a year. Thereafter, had it not been the opposition of his cousin, Robert Cecil, the Earl of Salisbury, he might have leaped to the supreme power.

There are two possible explanations of Salisbury's bitter-end opposition to Bacon's aspirations. According to Bacon, Salisbury was afraid of him—afraid that once his remedies were adopted, Salisbury's "small wares and petty points of cunning" would automatically become obsolete. According

---

8   The author had made a mark in his manuscript that this paragraph should be rewritten. We did not change the original text.

9   It is interesting to note the failed referendum in 2014 for Scotland to leave the United Kingdom, despite a strong independence movement (45% voted to leave).

to Salisbury, on the other hand, Bacon's remedies were completely unworkable in the world as it was then constituted, however attractive they might seem on paper. Nor did he propose to convert this court into a laboratory for trying them out. However, for his present purpose, which was simply to trap and disarm his cousin, he gave the latter the impression that he too had been converted to his remedies.

Thus, in March 1606, when the Solicitor General's place fell vacant, he made Bacon think that if he fulfilled certain conditions, he would be promoted to it. At first, Bacon was rather suspicious of the offer and asked for a pledge in writing. But the Little Beagle was convincing. "I am no dealer of holy water, but noble and real," Salisbury declared. "I will raise you, cousin, and when I have resolved to raise a man, I am more careful of him than of myself." And Bacon, preoccupied as he was with his great schemes, believed him.

Thus after some 15 years in the wilderness, Bacon finally had his foot securely on the ladder, or so it seemed. And even before there had been public confirmation of his appointment, he began to surround himself with extraordinary pomp and circumstance. "In fame of learning," he used to say, "the flight will be slow without some feathers of ostentation." But in this case, he seems to have been indulging his old weakness for celebrating his triumph before they happened.

Seven years before, at the death of his brother Anthony, he had inherited his father's estate at Gorhambury. Since then he had been so poor that he had had to sell "the skirts" of the estate so as "to preserve the body." But now, with an apparently firm commitment for the Solicitor's office, and with the promise of a substantial income of 3,000£ per annum, he not only recovered these "skirts," but also began to plan elaborate improvements upon them. The pondyards, about a mile from his father's old manor, would be turned into a "place of pleasure," and Verulum House, the headquarters for his research college, would be erected near it.

At the same time, he would expand his retinue into a large establishment rivalled only by the King's. It numbered now at most only about 15 or 20 men. But he had them dressed in Spanish leather boots (he could not tolerate the strong-smelling neats leather that was more commonly used), and the liveries that he designed for them would become more popular with gentlemen servants everywhere than the King's. But, by all odds, the most important innovation at this time was his marriage. For three years now, Bacon had been courting Alice Barnham, the daughter of the widow of a rich London alderman. His prospective mother-in-law had complained of his poverty and lack of prospects. But now with the promise of a promotion in hand, all such objections were waived.

The wedding took place on May 10, 1606, two months after the death of the former Solicitor General. It was held in St. Marylebone Chapel, located in the northern suburbs of London. And a brilliant affair it was! The bride was so well dressed that the spectators thought her whole dowry had been piled on her, her farthingale being heavily laden with silver and gold ornaments. Bacon himself was even more resplendent. As one observer said, "he was clad from top to toe in purple." The couple stood under an arch of drawn swords held by the groomsmen. After the vows were taken, the bridesmaids scattered rosemary, according to the custom of the time, and the groomsmen kissed the bride. Bacon was triumphant.

When someone questioned the extravagance of his men's liveries, he replied, proudly, "Sir, I am all of a piece. If the head be lifted up, the inferior parts of the body must be too." There was only one blemish in this bright tapestry. This was the absence of Salisbury, Bacon's cousin and patron, without whom there would have been no wedding at all. Ignoring this absence, and all its possible implications, Bacon graciously welcomed the three knights whom Salisbury had sent in his stead. "If I cannot have my Lord of Salisbury in person, which I had hoped," he said, "I will have him at least in a representative body."

So far not much has been said about Bacon's romantic side, if any. So now it is appropriate to see what he expected out of a marriage and what he actually got. In the first place, few men of this passionate age were so utterly devoid of passion as Bacon. "You may observe" he noted self-consciously in his *Essays*, "that amongst all the great and worthy persons either ancient or modern, there is not one that hath been transported to the mad degree of love." Sex, as such, meant nothing to him—"as if man, made for the contemplation of heaven and all noble objects should do nothing but kneel before a little idol."

On the other hand he undoubtedly had great need for the companionship of a devoted wife. Almost from start to finish of his extraordinary career, he was under great nervous tension. On two occasions when the tension subsided, he suffered from an ailment which we now call emotional fatigue,[10] its symptom, "a disposition to melancholy and distaste after sleeps, strife at meats, strangeness, clouds, etc." Had he acquired a wife with whom he "could communicate those secrets which troubled him most" he reflected later, such disorders could have been avoided. "Certainly, if a man would give it a hard phrase, those that want [companions] to open themselves unto are like cannibals of their own hearts."

How well did Alice Barnham fill the bill for these needs? From what little is known of her, we would say that she was almost totally inadequate, and that she was no more to him after the marriage than she was before, "a handsome maiden to my liking," an ornament with a modest dowry and nothing more. For one thing, there was an age barrier. She was 14, while Bacon was 45. For another thing, she seems to have been like her mother, empty-headed[11] and garrulous. When Bacon became Lord Chancellor and Lord St. Albans, the court gossips asked why she had made so little mark as compared with Lady Darby, the wife of the former Lord Chancellor. The answer was that "Lady Darby's wit lay backward [in her modesty] while my Lady St. Alban's lay forward, viz, in her tongue."

Again, like her mother, she seems to have been something of a goad and a nag. Instead of comforting him in his great and risky schemes (which no one could have argued him out of anyway), she urged him to forget them and to concentrate on the more conventional means to success. As a matter of fact, the mother-in-law was herself something more than he had bargained for. When she was not trying to exploit Bacon in her perennial feud with Sir John Pakington, her second husband, she amused herself by stirring up feuds between him and Lady Alice.

At one point, this meddling got so bad that Bacon had to order her out of the house. "I shall not suffer you to be an author or occasion of dissension between your daughter and [myself]" he said, "having seen so much of this in yourself." As for receiving Alice "if she be cast off," "it is much more likely we have occasion to receive you, being cast off," he said. She could return home, only "if she bore a mind of concord and love."

---

10 Today we would more likely refer to this as "burnout" or "burnout syndrome."

11 Spedding, the Bacon editor and scholar, suggested Bacon did not know Alice's age when he married her.

As we have seen, Bacon was a skillful manager so long as he put his mind to it. ("It is one of the best bonds in the wife, if she thinks her husband wise.") So in its early years, at least, he had no difficulty in ruling over this tempestuous household. Three months after the wedding, he told Sir Thomas Hoby, a friend, "I thank God I have not taken a thorn out of my foot to put it into my side. For as my estate is somewhat amended, so I have no other circumstances of complaint." Yet 15 years later, when his fortunes took a sudden downward turn, Alice would become a thorn, indeed, and he would regret that he had not built his home on a more substantial basis.

Meanwhile, the companionship that he could not find in his wife, he found among the few men who shared his belief in the conquest of nature—such men as Tobie Matthew and Bishop Andrewes. But these he saw rarely, Matthew being in exile abroad and Andrewes being occupied in church politics, "disputing between Kings and Popes." And from time to time, he sought the companionship of others like them.

Thus, when he was advised that Isaac Casaubon, the great French historian, also shared his interest in scientific research, he wrote to him at once to "communicate to me your own plans and occupations. For I ever think that this intercommunion of pursuits conduces more to friendship" than any other thing. My grand design, he explained, is "to draw the sciences out of their hiding places into the light . . . How great an enterprise this is, and with what small helps I have attempted it, you will perhaps learn hereafter." Casaubon (apparently), did not respond to this gesture. However, with every passing year, Bacon's disciples would increase both in numbers and in fervor. No matter how he might be discredited with the world at large, a solid corps of them would always worship him.

❦

Following his marriage to Alice Barnham, Bacon waited expectantly for the announcement of his appointment as Solicitor General. But for some reason that he did not understand, the appointment was delayed. He waited one month, two months, four months, and still no appointment. Bacon was embarrassed. Having spread his feathers, enlarged his retinue, and married in expectation of the office, he was now, as he put it, "a common gaze and a speech."

In a later case, almost exactly similar, when Bacon had tried unsuccessfully to become Master of the Court of Wards and Liveries, and bought new liveries for his men in expectation of the position, a court wit remarked that "Sir Walter [Cope], [Bacon's rival] has got the Wards, Sir Francis, the Liveries." Now, under heavy pressure from his mother-in-law and others, Bacon appealed over Salisbury's head to the King for a position that he thought he should have had at least 12 years before.

Over a year later, on June 25, 1607, his appointment was finally made official. But it was not until this time that he realized to what extent his cousin had trapped him. This office, Bacon had remarked, was "no great thing." But Salisbury stripped it of "its outward ornament and inward comforts." Worse yet, Salisbury bound Bacon to himself in such a way that it was impossible for him to demonstrate his new remedies. On the one hand, Bacon later told the King, he was tied like a hawk to another's fist—"a hawk that might sometimes bait and proffer but could never fly." On the other hand he was so loaded down with routine duties that surely this office must be "one of the painfullest places in the Kingdom."

Thus Bacon was made to pay the price for his gullibility. Moreover, the question was now raised how he could be entrusted with the King's great affairs when he was so inept about his own. Yet after some reflection, this question didn't bother him very much. As Themistocles used to say, "he could not fiddle [play petty politics] but yet he could make a small town a great city." In any case, when he came to power, there would be no need for "fiddling." Nor did he doubt for a moment that this day was fast approaching. The Parliamentary stalemate continued with ever increasing acrimony on both sides. Sooner or later, Salisbury would be discredited. And then at last, "the lame man [Bacon] who sticks to the track will overtake the swift man [Salisbury] who leaves it."

Thereafter, he quickly readjusted his ruffled feathers and once more assumed his godlike assurances. Where formerly he had dealt with his cousin in the most servile manner, assuring him that "I know your fortune is not to need a hundred such as I am," he would now deal with him "in a habit of natural, but no ways perilous boldness." Henceforth indeed, he would always be like himself "in vivacity, invention and enterprise."

Under other circumstances, Bacon's defiance would have cost him dear. But Salisbury was now making such heavy weather of it with his old-fashioned remedies that by contrast, Bacon's medicine gained new lustre. In April 1608, the "Little Beagle" became Lord Treasurer, while still holding his other titles. At that time the debt stood at the unprecedented height of £1,000,000, and since Parliament would authorize no new revenue, it was constantly rising with an annual deficit of £83,000.

Nonetheless, the King was as extravagant as ever, maintaining separate courts for the Queen and the Prince of Wales and entertaining lavishly. "If the nation wants heirs to the throne," he declared, "they will have to pay for them." By finding new sources of income, on the one hand, and by enforcing economies in the King's household, on the other hand, Salisbury tried to bring the budget into balance. The King would still appear on public occasions with £500,000 of jewels on his person. But the equipages of his retinue, such as his trumpeters' banners, were to be renewed every four years instead of annually. The amount of food that could be eaten and the beer that could be drunk at his table was severely limited. And some of his deer parks were sold for revenue.

Yet despite all of his ingenuity and despite his occasional ruthlessness, Salisbury still could not balance the budget. After six months in his new office, it looked very much as though he would have to grasp the nettle and do what he would have liked very much not to do, namely, to summon Parliament and try once more to break the deadlock between the King and the nation's representatives.

In this desperate hour, Salisbury may have decided that Bacon's remedies were not so utopian after all. But if so, his change of heart came too late. One day at Gorhambury, Bacon received a summons to dine with Salisbury in Salisbury House, the latter's palace on the Strand that was said to outstrip the villas of the wealthiest Cardinals in Rome. The two men were to meet in any event the following day on a purely routine matter. But now, Salisbury hinted that he wanted to take Bacon into his confidence and to get his advice on the handling of the new Parliament.

Bacon, believing that now at last his hour had come, rushed to London. But hardly had he returned to Gray's Inn than he changed his mind.

Nonsense, he thought, the thing is too fantastic. His cousin was simply preparing another trap for him, and having suffered once for his gullibility, he would not do it again. Sitting down at his desk, he dashed off a polite, but sharp-edged note: "Though it please your Lordship to use me as a kinsmen, yet I cannot leave behind me the shape of a Solicitor. I thought it better manners to wait till tomorrow [at] what time I will wait on you. Your Lordship, being in so good a place to refresh yourself," you can dine alone.

Just how far Salisbury would have taken Bacon into his confidence on this occasion and how much of Bacon's counsel he would have adopted as his own, we don't know. But shortly afterwards, Salisbury made the greatest blunder of his life. His solution to the deadlock was to negotiate an agreement or "contract" by which the King would agree to make certain popular reforms in return for the retirement of the debt and a large annual appropriation. At first glance, this looked like something out of Bacon's book, and indeed, it was probably drawn from Bacon's blueprint for a perfect monarchy. One of the reforms called for the abolition of feudal vestiges and looked forward to a new age of nationalism—an age when men would no longer stop to ask whose tenants they were and by what feudal obligations they held their land, but would all rally to the Crown out of patriotism alone.

But instead of moving boldly into this new age with mutual understanding between the King and his people, Salisbury would do it with mutual enmity—with the King dragging his feet and haggling with his subjects like a fishmonger over the price of his leadership. When Bacon first heard about this plan, despite his own indirect share in it, he had no difficulty in seeing that it wouldn't work. As he later told the King, "To have your wants and particular necessities as it were hanged up in two tablets before the eyes of your Lords and Commons; to have all your courses which were wont to be held secret [which included the bills for the royal sheets, blankets, clothing and furnishings] now put into printed books; to contract still where might be the readiest payment and not the best bargain; to pretend even carriage between Your Majesty's rights and the ease of the people and satisfy neither—these courses and others [can do little but] turn your Majesty to inestimable prejudice."

Nor did Salisbury make his plan seem more palatable when he tried to force it through Parliament. He tried every "trick and cavillation" that he had learned in his two decades of experience in high places. He raised the terms of his contract, then he lowered them again. Repeatedly, he tried to speed up the long debate so that "all protraction in this so great and necessary a business might be avoided." Yet neither by these tactics nor by others could he conceal from the Commons the essential insincerity and hollowness of his proposal.

Throughout the entire debate, one member said, there remained "the doubt whether this contract was authentic as my Lord [of Salisbury] would have us believe, or burlesque, as some of our wise men suspect." After four months or so, even the King lost patience with his "Little Beagle."

"His Majesty hath now had patience with this assembly these seven years and from them received more disgraces, censures and ignominies than ever Prince did endure." James said, "our fame and actions have been tossed like tennis balls," and he had suffered renewed attacks of the gout. Yet the exchequer was still empty. "Your Lordship hath advised me to have patience. I cannot have asinine patience." If Salisbury succeeded in negotiating another Kingdom at such a price, he said he would not accept it.

Ordinarily, such a rebuke from the King would not have disturbed him very much. But this time, Salisbury was at the end of his rope and the possibility that his cousin might succeed where he failed did not make him any happier. For two years more he went through the motions of governing England. But his heart was not in it, and as his health broke, bit by bit, he let the reins slip from him. Even during his heyday, he had been a lonely, worrisome, often conscience-stricken figure, completely absorbed in his official papers. His wife, for whom he had had a deep affection, had died some years before the accession of King James, and he had never remarried. Pomp, wealth, and supreme success had not brought him happiness.

Oddly enough, Hatfield House, his new country seat, had just been finished. But he had no desire, apparently, to move into it. Drawing up his will, he expressed desire "to go without noise and vanity, out of this vale of misery as a man that has long been satisfied with terrestrial glory and now contemplates only heavenly joy." But, the King could not bear to part with this councillor who had served him so doggedly. Perhaps, also, he regretted his recent impatience with him. He sent him presents and on two visits tried to rally him. But to no avail. Salisbury died on May 24, 1612, at the youthful age of 48.

By this time, Salisbury had been almost totally discredited among his fellow courtiers. He was described as an unprincipled trimmer, "who juggled with religion, with the King, Queen, their children, with nobility, Parliament, with friends, foes and generally with all." Indeed, a letterwriter was astonished that so important a figure should be censured so widely and so soon after his death. Nobody had more reason to join this hostile chorus than Bacon, whose aspirations had so long been blocked by his late cousin. Yet when his turn came to pass judgment on him, unlike the others, he did not deny the essential integrity of the man, nor did he deny his great gifts within the conventional range.

"Now tell me truly," asked James, "what think you of your cousin that is gone?"

"Sir," Bacon replied, "since your Majesty charges me, I will give you such a character of him as if I were to write his story [history]. I do think he was no fit councillor to make your affairs better. But yet he was fit to have kept them from growing worse."

To which James replied "on my soul man! In the first, thou speakest like a true man; in the second, like a kinsman." When Bacon repeated this estimate of his cousin in his *Essays* (Second Edition), published the following October, it was said that Bacon "paints his little cousin to the life."

What Bacon was really trying to say by this witticism was that where Salisbury had failed by his "practical" methods, Bacon could succeed by his new-style remedies. Thus, he opened his second major campaign for the supreme power under the King. For five years now, his talent had been "so hidden that I did conceive Your Majesty may think it rather a kind of dullness or want of faith than modesty, if I should not come with my pitcher to Jacob's well as others do." During that period, he went on, "I have worked that Your Majesty might prevail in all your causes, and not merely prevail," but prevail "with satisfaction of the inner man"—that is to say, in accordance with Bacon's own principles.

Thus, when the King's causes were weak, Bacon sometimes put forward "that which was good to keep back that which was not so good." When his causes were downright bad, as with Salisbury's Great Contract scheme, Bacon perfunctorily went through the motions of supporting them, or sat on his hands, tactfully indicating his opposition to them. Thus, while Salisbury had been losing ground, Bacon had acquired "some [further] little reputation with the world." Now on the one hand, "no man can say but that I was a perfect and peremptory royalist. Yet every man makes me believe that I was never one hour out of credit with the lower house."

Never before had Bacon's otherwise impossible case seemed so plausible. However, the King had been so badly burned in his last encounter with the Parliament, that he had no stomach for another—either by the old-fashioned remedies or the new—and he postponed his decision as long as possible. Indeed, for the next year or so, he endeavored to balance his budget more or less by economy alone—with himself as acting Secretary of State, and Bacon temporarily sidetracked as a member of a financial commission to study the budget. However, if Salisbury could not discipline his extravagant habits, how could the King do it himself?

In February 1613, to celebrate his daughter's marriage to Frederick, the Elector Palatine of the Rhine, he ordered another extravaganza, with a new banqueting hall to be erected especially for it, with sea fights, floating castles and fireworks on the Thames, all totaling about £50,000. When the celebration was over, the king was so debt-ridden and his credit so low that his brewer refused to supply him with beer until an account of £16,000 had been settled. In desperation, he now agreed to give Bacon a chance to show what he could do with a new Parliament—but with reservations. Instead of making him Secretary of State, which would have clearly marked him as Salisbury's successor with supreme power, the King made him Attorney General, which was no more than a routine appointment up the ladder from Solicitor General. This appointment was confirmed on October 27, 1613.

If Bacon was disappointed by this, he did not show it. On the contrary, he acted as if he had all the authority he needed and gave minute instructions both to the King and to the court generally on what he would expect from them. About a year previously, he had published the new edition of his *Essays*, and here, in a highly condensed and palatable form, he had already announced the remedies that he would employ with the new Parliament. In one essay, "Of the True Greatness of Kingdoms and Estates," he had given a complete description of the imaginary government that he was now trying to make a reality.

As the ages rolled by and the world partially caught up with Bacon, this little book would prove suggestive to many statesmen. Even now, it did not lack admirers, particularly among the more visionary young Earls of the court. From his chaplain we get a picture of Bacon holding forth to his followers at Gorhambury. His "discourses" at table, the chaplain says, were much like his *Essays*. "They were rather more like oracles than discourses, which may be imputed either to the well-weighing of his sentences by the scales of truth and reason, or else to the reverence wherein he was commonly held. No man would contest with him."

The Earl of Dorset even went so far as to bring along a retainer, Sir Thomas Billingsley, "to remember and put down in writing" his most casual phrases. Yet, unfortunately for Bacon, these young Earls constituted only a small minority of the King's court.

"There is a general apprehension," wrote a letterwriter, "that little good is to be expected by this appointment." Like Salisbury, before them, many now feared that Bacon would prove to be "a dangerous instrument."

Meanwhile, Bacon was having difficulty with the King. Bacon had suggested that the new Parliament be summoned for some "great reform measure and not merely for money." The King had expressed his concern about this. "But what about the debt? How will you pay it?"

"The debt," Bacon replied, will be repaid by a "skillful compound of a number of ingredients," as becomes a scientific cure, and not "by any one fine extract or strong water," or patent medicine. James must have patience. Otherwise "you will prejudice your honor, safety, and profit." When the King still expressed his doubts about the new remedy, Bacon gave him this now familiar, but then unconventional advice. "It is no new thing," he said, "for the greatest of Kings to be in debt," nor for the greatest of councillors either. He mentioned Leicester (Elizabeth's favorite), Essex, Salisbury, and he may have been tempted to include himself—"all in debt, yet it was no manner of diminution to their power and greatness." Nor should you "trouble or vex your Majesty's mind" with this problem. "When Moses took the children of Israel to the land of promise," Bacon continued suggestively, "that land had no great river to water it like Egypt, but had to depend on the rains. Whereby I gather, God preferreth sometimes uncertainties before certainties, because they teach a more immediate dependence upon his providence."

CHAPTER FIVE

FLIRTING WITH MEPHISTO

"Neither let any man think that herein he tempteth God.
For the sun entereth into sinks and is not defiled."
                                        —*Bacon, Religious Meditations*

During the winter of 1613–14, there were moments when it looked very much as if the King would adopt Bacon's plan for a perfect monarchy *in toto*. In this belief, at any rate, Bacon began to dream of his other great enterprise, his research college, which he was slowly building at Gorhambury. Since his last public appeal for this enterprise, he had not said very much about it. In 1612, in his suit for the office of Attorney General, he had referred to it as a thing of such magnitude that it could "occupy all my thoughts" and had promised to "make it much more manifest to your Majesty and the world."

Meanwhile, a rich merchant, Sutton, had died, leaving a large endowment (among other bequests) for a grammar school to be established in his name. A question had been raised as to the legality of this foundation. If it was found to be illegal, then the crown could receive £100,000, which Bacon thought might conceivably be applied to his own enterprise. "If this foundation be perfect and good in law," he told the King, "I would never advise any course of profit that is not grounded on a right." But "if there be a right," whereby the disposal of these funds is in your "power and grace," then they would be much better used for setting up a research college in the great universities than for a new grammar school.

On the one hand, he went on, there are "already too many grammar schools." On the other hand (as he had said before), without research the sciences that are taught in the Universities will remain "superficial" and "become but pretty and compendious habits of practice." From past experience, Bacon knew of course that the professors would never tolerate such a novel enterprise in their midst. Yet, once again, he was anxious to get it thoroughly discussed both in the Universities and also in the Privy Council.

This proposal was based on so many remote contingencies that the King paid no attention to it. However, even on the political front, Bacon's plans began to lose ground. When he had first begun to lecture the King on his new remedies for this "repair of His Majesty's exchequer," the King had been very attentive. These lectures, the latter had agreed, were not "tricks" or "novelties," but "true passages of business."

But for some reason or other, the lectures had failed to strike home. Perhaps, it was because Bacon had overestimated the capacity of his royal pupil. Time and again, both as King of Scotland and now as King of England as well, he had resolved to rule as a model King—only to backslide again on the eve of action. On the other hand, perhaps, it was because Bacon's own standards were so absurdly high and impractical.

Certainly, Bacon had not won the King's confidence by these lectures as he had hoped to do. In the King's presence where he should have been most ingratiating, he was stiff and ill-at-ease. Even when he wrote him a thank-you note, he would draft it three or four times out of his stock of approved compliments. Little wonder then that the King admired his new Attorney General for his wisdom, but, as yet, didn't really like him very much. As soon as Bacon had bowed out of the presence chamber, he would consult with Robert Carr, his young Scottish favorite who was much easier to take on all counts.

Carr had his debut at court some seven years before by falling under his horse and breaking his leg at a tilting match. The King was instantly struck by the youth's noble bearing and manner. During Carr's convalescence, he personally taught him Latin. Afterwards, he permitted him to dress his royal person, to take dictation, and to perform such other duties around the household as were appropriate for the King's favorite. Before this, Carr had been nothing more than an adventurer like a hundred others at court, the son of a Scottish laird, but otherwise undistinguished. Now his rise was so meteoric that he soon outshone all the other courtiers. In 1608, the King gave him the manor that he had confiscated from Raleigh; in 1611, he made him a Viscount; in 1613 he created him Earl of Somerset. And it was with this rank that he emerged as the new leader of the anti-Bacon faction.

Had Bacon really established his perfect government, Somerset's career would have been nipped in the bud. For "neither in jest nor in earnest" would the King have given "countenance or ear" to "flatterers or sycophants" anywhere within his inner circle. Also, the King would have adopted the rule of King David "that there shall be no deceitful person dwell in my house." But, he had no authority to enforce this rule, and while he was laboring to raise the idealism of the courtiers, Somerset was "buzzing around like a fly," trying to lower it again. "[Revels] are fit in their seasons," Bacon wrote, "but if they shall become too frequent, they will lose their repute and become arguments of lightness rather than of recreation."

The revels introduced by Somerset answered neither of Bacon's specifications. They were unseasonable on the eve of a new Parliament, and as to their frequency, it would seem that court life was now one continuous debauch. Women affected "yellow bands, dusted hair, curls crisped, sleek skins and open breasts beyond accustomed attire, while men became unmannerly and unruly like Sir Edward Sackville who left a dinner given by the Lord Mayor of London in his honor to put a young lady to the squeak" in an upstairs apartment.

Worse yet, in the wake of this prolonged debauch, came a great increase in duelling. Within the space of one year there were half a dozen duels. Lord Bruce was killed, the above-named Sackville was wounded, a barrister at Gray's Inn lost three fingers, and another barrister—his rival—had his nose bitten off. Two other groups of young noblemen had planned duels to take place on the continent, and these no doubt would have resulted in further fatalities, had not the King had the participants arrested as they disembarked.

However Bacon may have reconciled himself to Somerset's other innovations, clearly, he would not tolerate duelling. "Life is grown too cheap in these times," he told the King. "We are losing the flower of your youth," and all because of a "false sense of honor and credit." Everybody agrees that Greece and Rome were the "most valiant and generous nations of the world.

Yet they knew nothing of duelling. If we are ever to emerge from the Dark Ages into a comparable era, clearly we also must get rid of it."[12]

The King agreed wholeheartedly with Bacon. He had such a horror of violence and bloodshed that he could hardly hold a naked sword in his hand for ceremonial purposes without blanching. At Bacon's suggestion he issued a proclamation prohibiting all duels, or challenges to duels, upon pain of perpetual banishment from approach to the courts of the King, Queen, and Prince. The drafting of this proclamation he had entrusted to the verbose Earl of Northampton who made it so vague that nobody took it seriously.

But in a test case between a couple of "base" mechanical persons (he would have preferred a case involving noblemen so as to emphasize its seriousness), Bacon made a very powerful argument for the proclamation—an argument that the lords of the Council had printed and circulated "as a thing very meet and worthy to be remembered and known unto the world." Here once again, Bacon's remedy was premature. It would be 250 years or so before duelling could be successfully outlawed from respectable society. Yet imaginative Bacon was convinced that his proclamation was a great success.

As the opening day of the new Parliament approached, the King became increasingly nervous about the kind of reception they would give him. "If your majesty had heard and seen the thunder of the bells and the lightning of the bonfires for [the birth] of your grandchild, you would say there is little cause to doubt the affections of the people," Bacon told him reassuringly. If you will "proceed in a more familiar, and yet more princely manner," your meeting with Parliament will be both peaceful and successful.

But Somerset and the men around him were frightened. In place of Bacon's high-minded strategy, they would have the King adopt Salisbury's or perhaps still another strategy, more openly tyrannical. They would rig the elections so as to fill the House of Commons with the King's hand-picked supporters (known henceforth as "Undertakers") and then use these men to push through appropriation bills for the Crown. "Why should [opposition] blackguards try to dictate to their Prince? Let their Prince dictate to them," Somerset said.

---

12 In the original manuscript, this last sentence was not contained in the preceding quotation. Based on context, the editors surmised it should be included in the quotation, as it appears here.

Bacon bitterly opposed this counter-proposal. Such practices, he said, will backfire, "increasing animosities and oppositions. They will [put] whatsoever shall be done in evil conceit amongst your people in general afterwards." But the King's confidence in Bacon was now on the decline. Not only did he authorize the use of this "strange new kind of beasts called Undertakers," but he also asked Bacon to join with them. By this time, there was so little left of Bacon's plans for a perfect monarchy that he would have been well advised to abandon them altogether and retire into the background again. Yet, ignoring the Undertakers, he carried on as though nothing had happened.

In his opening speech before the new Parliament on April 8, James struck a lofty note. Parliament had been convened, he said, to celebrate the birth of an heir to his daughter and her husband, a Count of the Holy Roman Empire, and to discuss the increased English interests in that area resulting therefrom. Slowly then and gingerly, the King worked up to the disputed question of an appropriation for the Crown. This appropriation, he pointed out, had nothing to do with his personal needs. In response to suggestions made at their previous meeting, he had separated the budget for his household expenses from that of the public service.

But in connection with the latter, he now had a very ambitious program, both domestic and foreign. This speech, it seems, had been drafted for him by Bacon, and as long as the King stuck to it, he probably had his audience with him. But unfortunately, he not only read the text, but also the notes or private precautions that Bacon had provided for his guidance. This, of course, made the whole performance seem contrived and insincere. "Your Majesty must put off the person of merchant and rest upon the person of a King," Bacon had told him.

"I am now offering you certain graces and favors," James repeated mechanically, "not in the way of merchandising which I will not allow, nor cannot abide to hear of but of mere good will." Again Bacon had cautioned him: "I think it a thing inestimable for your Majesty's safety and service that you once part with your Parliament with love."

"I would rather have the love of my people than their money," echoed the King, adding that he hoped this Parliament would be known to posterity as "the Parliament of Love."

Despite this blunder, the King might have got away with it, had not his Undertakers "stumbled on the threshold," as Bacon had predicted they would. For now, without even giving the House a chance to discuss the King's speech or the program contained in it, they tried to force the issue on his appropriations bill. The members resented this action. We are being betrayed from within by Undertakers, they said, adding that such men had no place in a free assembly. One member compared them with the "powder-traitors," the conspirators who had tried by gunpowder to destroy the King and Parliament nine years before. Only they are worse, he said. For the "powder-traitors" would have blown us up by force, while the "Undertakers" are working more subtly and in secret to the same end. All other business was now forgotten while a Committee of the Whole House was organized to track down and expel the offenders.

At this critical juncture, Bacon tried to abandon his role as one of the King's high officers, and to appear, as in former years, as a popular Parliamentary leader. But here for the first time, he came face to face with the contradictions of his new position. Bacon had been returned to the House of Commons, not merely by one borough, but by three, including the University of Cambridge. But if the "Undertakers," the King's special agents, could not be trusted in the House, one member asked, why should the Attorney General, the King's chief law officer? But this member was probably some newcomer who did not know of Bacon's reputation as a disinterested reformer. While a ruling was made that henceforth no Attorney General could sit in the House of Commons, Bacon himself was honored by being named as the single exception to this ruling. With this difficulty out of the way, he now employed all his great imaginative gifts and all his power of persuasion to smooth the troubled waters.

By introducing five bills, he painted another picture of the perfect government he would create for them if only they would have confidence in the King. One of these bills embodied a reform that he had been advocating ever since the Queen's time—the "reformation of the laws" with the repeal of "snares" and the purging of "multiplicities" for the better "execution of those laws that are wholesome and necessary." If he could have convinced the House that he could really establish this new reform any better than he had established his earlier reforms, then, perhaps, they might have given the King another chance. But as matters stood, they had no such conviction.

Thus, instead of helping the King by these proposals, Bacon only damaged himself.

As the days passed, instead of becoming more loving and responsive, the House of Commons became ever more unruly. As one courtier put it, they were converted from a "grave council" into a "cockpit," and "many sat there that were more fit to have been among roaring boys than in that assembly." Angry letters were exchanged between the House and the palace, and there was much comment about the King's prerogative. Up to this point, the King had behaved with unprecedented forbearance. But public discussion of his prerogative was his weak point. When one member called him a tyrant, and another referred flippantly to Somerset as "a spaniel to the King and a wolf to the people," he completely lost his head.

Tyrannically answering the change of tyranny, he had the offender arrested and sent to the Tower. At much the same time, he issued an ultimatum to the House that if they didn't use their liberties more modestly, he would send them home. Scornfully, the House rejected the ultimatum. So on June 7, after two months of futile wrangling, Parliament was formally dissolved. Henceforth, it would become known, not as the "Parliament of Love," which was the King's wish, but, more appropriately as the "Addled Parliament."

Following Bacon's failure to convert him into a perfect monarch, James took those fateful and irreversible steps which 26 years hence would bring about a national uprising and 9 years after that, the execution of his son, Charles I, on a scaffold erected in front of James' Banqueting House. James simply could not believe that the Addled Parliament had truly reflected the temper of his people. When a councillor suggested that since Parliament had failed to provide for his upkeep, by appropriations, the people should do this by voluntary subscriptions or "benevolences," he promptly accepted the plan. Hopefully, then, circulars announcing the subscription were printed and sent out to local officials. As an example and incentive, highly placed courtiers deposited some £23,000 worth of plate and jewels at the King's Jewel House.

But when the contributions came in from the counties, they were pitifully inadequate. After the first six months of the campaign, the collections totalled only about one-quarter of the annual appropriations that would normally have been voted by Parliament. Some counties gave nothing at all. Obviously, the people's love for James was at a very low ebb. Nor did this campaign for voluntary subscription increase it any. In Somersetshire, a Puritan rector named Peacham, had written but not delivered a sermon, referring to James as a liar, a miser, and a tyrant and predicting his eventual overthrow by popular revolt. All such critics of the King were so ruthlessly punished that the subscriptions could hardly be called voluntary any more.

Thus, in the unequal warfare between Bacon's imaginary government and Somerset's real one, Somerset had won the field, and Bacon as Attorney General now had to enforce measures that were completely at odds with the ones he had proposed. In the matter of free speech, he believed in giving "moderate liberty" so that "griefs and discontentments" might safely "evaporate." "For he that turneth the humors back and maketh the wound bleed inwards, endangereth malign ulcers and pernicious importhumations." Yet so long as the King ruled by a system of tyranny rather than according to his own blueprints, free speech was obviously an impossible luxury.

By this same nightmarish logic, Bacon could also see that they would have to make an "example" out of Peacham, the incendiary rector. Yet, obviously, he had no stomach for this business and by contrast to Peacham's other prosecutors, he tried to humanize it as much as possible. After all, in predicting an uprising, Peacham had written nothing that he had not written himself. Someday, perhaps, he too would be caught up by the same logic. Thus, in the preliminary examinations where the others put Peacham to the "manacles" to get their information, Bacon got his simply by talking to him and by closely studying "the motions of his face" and "gestures." During the trial, Bacon let it be known that "if the fellow submit himself, he shall have no great harm," and after the trial, despite Peacham's persistent refusal to submit, Bacon still tried to get a pardon for him. But it was too late. The poor rector had been so sorely abused in the torture chamber that he died before Bacon could make amends to him.

A less inspired and more realistic reformer than Bacon would have been flattened by such a defeat as this, and probably have retired then and there. Even Bacon must have had many second thoughts about staying on in the service under these conditions. "It is a strange desire to seek power and to lose liberty, or to seek power over others and to lose liberty over a man's self," he had written earlier, probably after a similar setback under Salisbury.

Yet dwelling in a new era—mentally, at least—when all man's "troubled relations" would be conducted on a more reasonable basis, he couldn't take this new tyranny very seriously. Sooner or later, he thought, the King would come to his senses and see the situation as it really was.

When this happened, two things would follow. First, he would cast this insubstantial Somerset into the discard and give Bacon the supreme power. Then, under Bacon's direction, the dream of the perfect monarchy would at last become a reality. For he still believed that with increased "power and place as the commanding ground" his impossible plan could be "put into act." He did not have to wait long before he would be given another opportunity to prove how wrong this assumption really was.

�֍

Somerset's downfall was one of the most incredible of all the incredible events of King James' reign. Yet it did not come altogether as a surprise to Bacon. "It is a strange thing to note the excess of this passion [of love]," he had written. ". . . For whosoever esteemeth too much of amorous affection quitteth both riches and wisdom." In these two sentences, he had already summed up the strange story that now unfolded before his eyes.

The lady in the case was Frances Howard, Lady Essex. She was connected with the most powerful families at the court, with the Lord Privy Seal and the Lord Chamberlain, and she was the recent bride of the third Earl of Essex, the faceless son of Elizabeth's favorite. She was a fabulous flirt, described by court gossips as "the most impudent woman that lived." For once she had set her mind to win the King's favor, they said, "there was no hope with her."

The Somerset-Frances romance began under the bright candles of the palace ballroom. It was consummated at secret meetings in the dismal lodgings of Hammersmith. It was presided over from first to last by professional witches, retained by Lady Frances for this purpose. No one knew how far this passionate affair had gone save Somerset's closest friend and adviser, Sir Thomas Overbury. More particularly, no one except Overbury knew that Somerset was determined to have his flame divorced from Essex (which was a very difficult thing to do in those days) and to take Lady Frances as his lawful bride.

Had Overbury agreed with Somerset in this plan, this romance would hardly have been noted in the pages of history. However, Overbury not only disagreed with his lord, but apparently also threatened to disclose all the details of their illicit relations—a disclosure that would have rendered Somerset's marriage plan legally impossible. To remove Overbury from the scene, Somerset had him framed into an act of disobedience to the King for which he was sent to the Tower. Still unsure of themselves, Lady Frances, apparently, with Somerset's knowledge and consent, arranged with Overbury's jailer that he should be poisoned. At first, the poison was administered in small doses—in special jellies and ointments just strong enough to make him sick. Gradually, the dosage was increased to lethal proportions. Overbury died on September 15, 1613. Three days after this, Lady Frances was divorced from Essex, and three months after that, the lovers were married amid festivities of almost regal proportions.

Yet somehow, the ghost of Overbury lived on to haunt the couple. In 1614, one of Overbury's poems, "The Wife, Now a Widow," was published posthumously; in it were clear allusions to the circumstances of their romance. Meanwhile, anonymous letters had begun to circulate suggesting that Overbury was the victim of foul play and vaguely pointing the finger at the highly placed couple. Somerset lived in terror with his guilt written all over him. The King complained of his "continual dogged sullen behaviour." He also complained that his favorite had exceeded his license by annoying the King at "unseasonable hours" as though he were deliberately trying to break the other's rest.

Nonetheless, it was almost the perfect crime. Shortly after Overbury's death, Somerset had secured a blanket pardon for any crime that he had committed or might commit in the future. Moreover, the few people who had actual knowledge of this crime, including the Lieutenant of the Tower, remained silent, either because they were implicated in it or because they were afraid to bring charges against such "great persons." Even when this new evidence was in hand, implicating Lady Frances as the murderess and Somerset as an accessory before the fact, the King was reluctant to bring them to trial. They were under the influence of witches, he suggested. Hence, they could not be held accountable for what they had done.

King James had always been very prone to blame his misfortunes on imaginary witches of one kind or another. But, in this case, it was undeniably true that Lady Frances had employed two professional witches to help her win the favorite. One of these witches was Mrs. Ann Turner, a fashionable dressmaker with a large following at court, who secretly practiced "sorcery and enchantment" on the side. The other was Dr. Simon Forman, a graduate physician of Jesus College, Cambridge, who had had his license revoked and had been locked up in the Tower for the same illegal practice.

These two had provided Lady Frances with (1) "an enchanted nutmeg" or love potion, and (2) a series of obscene images, designed variously to inflame Somerset's passion towards her and to fool her first husband. Their actual connection with the murder plot seems to have been rather remote. But it was enough to warrant their trial as accessories before the fact. Moreover, when Sir Edward Coke, the Lord Chief Justice, took charge of Mrs. Turner's prosecution, he made full use of her supposedly demonic character.

Coke's wrath against Mrs. Turner was increased, it was believed, by the fact that his wife, Lady Hatton, was also one of her clients. Mrs. Turner, he told the jury, was a whore, a bawd, a sorcerer, and "the daughter of the Devil Forman." She was guilty of all the seven deadly sins. Then, in a more subdued form, he asked her to repent—to become a servant to Jesus Christ and to pray to Him to cast out the devils from her bosom. The "Devil Forman" had lied prior to the trial and so was spared a similar ordeal.

The trial, which was held in the Guildhall, was a great public success. Seats were sold at the exorbitant price of £10 each, and special box sets for £50. Yet so many crowded into them that the scaffolding gave way and many of the spectators were injured. The execution that followed the conviction was also a public success. The hangman wore yellow bands and yellow cuffs in mockery of the color yellow that Mrs. Turner had done so much to make fashionable at court.

It should be mentioned here that Bacon's attitude towards the witches was in marked contrast to Sir Edward Coke's. Instead of being horrified by them, he was fascinated. What interested him was not the theological delusion that they could communicate with the Devil, but rather the very real psychological influence that they exercised over their patrons. Indeed, he had already made, or soon would make, some scientific experiments on this point. These experiments indicated that if a man wanted to win a woman, or get a job, or recover from an illness, his "constant belief" in his ultimate success could be strengthened by the so-called witches. And so, the man's own efforts towards these goals would become that much bolder and more vigorous. Thus, Bacon concluded, the trouble with witchcraft lay not so much with its methods as with the ends, which were almost always depraved and evil.

But suppose a man of good will could invent some method by which he could strengthen his subjects in their "just and virtuous ends"—a method as effective as the one used by witches for evil ends. That man would surely be a great benefactor of mankind. Moreover, by this invention, he might conceivably remove all witches from the scene. "For if the ends of our actions are good and the resolutions of our mind for obtaining them fixed and constant, the mind will directly mould itself at once to all kinds of virtue," and be proof against evil influence.

This, in effect, was what Bacon had been vainly trying to do with the King ever since the latter's accession to the English throne—namely, to bewitch him into becoming a perfect monarch. Hitherto, it had been obvious to everybody but Bacon himself that his ends were too high and his means inadequate to his ends. But now, oddly enough, he did succeed in getting the King to turn over a new leaf, particularly in his attitude towards witches.

During his apprenticeship on the Scottish throne, James had once accused witches of raising a storm in the North Sea for the sole purpose of delaying his marriage to Princess Anne of Denmark: without a pang of conscience, he had two groups of them summarily tried, convicted, and burned for this alleged offense. Now he became so cautious that he would permit few convictions of alleged witches until he had personally examined the evidence against them. Either he had the accused brought to the palace, or he would make special trips to their homes. But the more cases he examined, the more he realized that what looked like "demonical seizures" were really only fits or frauds. Thomas Fuller about 50 years later wrote: "King James receding from what he had written in his *Demonology* grew first diffident of, and then flatly to deny the workings of witches and devils as but falsehoods and delusions." In 1618, the witchhunts suddenly ceased and would continue in abeyance until James' death in 1625.

Meanwhile, on the political front, the King had withdrawn his objections to the prosecution of Somerset and his wife—which, in Bacon's eyes, at least, indicated that once more he wanted to rule as a perfect monarch. As Bacon later said, James wanted to "show the world, as if it were written in a sunbeam, that his affections royal are above his affections private" and "that his favors and nearness about him are not like Popish sanctuaries [for the protection of malefactors]."

On November 2, 1615, which was less than a week before Mrs. Turner's trial, the King had Somerset stripped of his robes and ornaments, and moved from his palace chambers to the Tower. Lady Frances was pregnant at this time. But as soon as she had delivered her child, she was sent to join him. Within a month, Bacon was called in to replace Coke as chief prosecutor. Earlier, in a long letter to the King, Somerset had protested the indignity of being cross-examined by Coke. But the King was firm about this, as he was later about his appointment of Bacon. In answer to Somerset, he wrote: "When in my conscience I have set down a course, to change it at the instance of the party were little for my honor…. In a nature of this business, I have nothing to look unto but first my conscience before God and next my reputation in the eyes of the whole world. If I can find one man stricter than another in point of examination, I am bound in conscience to employ him."

As has been said before, Bacon had never reconciled himself to the victory of Somerset's tyranny over his own regime. Indeed, as with his former defeat at the hands of his cousin Salisbury, he had gone out of his way to show his contempt for his rival. Two years before, Somerset had tried to make Bacon pay him for his promotion as Attorney General. Even by the rules of palace politics then prevailing, there was no justice in Somerset's claim. "It was your sole act," Bacon later told the King. "Somerset, when he knew your Majesty had resolved upon it, thrust himself into the business for a fee."

A few months later, however, at the time of Somerset's marriage to Lady Frances, Bacon found an ingenious way of placating Somerset and preserving his own colossal dignity at one and the same time. Somerset had indicated that the wedding presents would be accepted in payment of favors past, present, or future, and the courtiers generally outdid themselves to make this a happy occasion for him. Ralph Winwood, soon to be confirmed as Secretary of State, gave the couple a brace of fine horses for their carriage; others loaded them with plate, and large well filled purses. Bacon also went to great expense, spending more than £2,000 in their honor.

He gave them a public banquet, the chief attraction of which was a dramatic piece entitled *The Masque of the Flowers*. It was a tasteful tidbit, if not written by him, at least produced according to his specifications—with music "loud and cheerful," "with light specially colored and varied" and "inoffensive dancing." As it turned out, it was more of a tribute to Bacon, the impresario, than to his guests of honor. For it had been written, rehearsed and staged by some dozen of his barristers of Gray's Inn, and in the remarkably short space of three weeks. "[This] could not have been done," they told him, "but that every man's exceeding love and respect for you gave him wings to overtake Time, which is the swiftest of things."

As Somerset's prosecutor, on the other hand, Bacon showed no trace of rancor or revenge. On the contrary, he used this occasion to illustrate just how criminal cases should be conducted. According to his chaplain, this was "to look upon the example severely, but upon the person with pity and compassion." So now, when the Lord Steward took his place as presiding officer of the Star Chamber and the Somersets were seated in the prisoners' box, he gave the latter every consideration. In his opening sentence, he assured them that "we shall not seek [dramatic] prizes or to blazen our names in blood or to carry the day otherwise than upon facts." The charge against them, he said, was very serious. "It is murder; it is murder by poison; it is murder committed upon the King's prisoner in the tower—and if I can prove it, it is murder under the color of friendship."

The case against Somerset was complicated somewhat in that the precise degree of his guilt was unknown. So the manner of "charging" him was moderated as it might not make him too "odious" for possible clemency by the King. In Lady Frances's case there were fewer mysteries. But he called the attention of the judges to "her youth, her sex, her noble family, yea her provocations"—that is, her association with the professional witches. He asked that she be escorted back and forth from the prisoner's box by an axman—a courtesy usually reserved for defendants in treason cases rather than in murder cases—and over Coke's objection, the court granted his request. A letterwriter said, "She was used with more respect than usual, nothing being aggravated against her, nor any invective used, but only touching the main offense of murder." Almost universally, it seems, Bacon's handling of the case was applauded.

Following the conviction of the Somersets (they were sentenced to be hanged, though three months later, this sentence was commuted to life imprisonment), Bacon began to dream once more of establishing his own regime. The office from which he now proposed to do this was the Lord Chancellor's—in point of dignity and authority the highest office in the realm, and the same office that his father had held (but with the lesser title of Lord Keeper) for so long under Queen Elizabeth—a point that he also considered worth noting.

As Lord Chancellor, of course, his burdens and responsibilities would be increased considerably. He would have to dispense the King's justice in the Court of Chancery, which was the high court of equity. Also through a subordinate officer, the Master of the Rolls, he would have custody of the Archives, and under the Great Seal, he would pass all charters, letters patent, and state papers. Also he would have to preside over the Star Chamber, the House of Lords, and the Privy Council.

However, balanced against these burdensome duties, was the fact that he would have extraordinary access to the throne. As someone said earlier, he would be "the eye, the ear, the mouth, and the very heart of the prince." In sum, it would be impossible to imagine a better vantage point from which he could breathe life and substance into his blueprints, if that was really within his power. And if it wasn't, there was always his research college. He would now be earning £10,000 to 15,000 per year as compared with the £6,000 that he was earning as Attorney General; with this income, according to his original calculations, he should now be able to "complete the design."

This task would have been easier (he thought) if he could have worked directly with the King and without a favorite as a third party. But hardly did Somerset fall from grace when another pink-cheeked youngster stepped into his shoes. He was Sir George Villiers, formerly the King's cupbearer. If this was disappointing to Bacon, he did not show it. Indeed, almost before anybody else had realized what had happened, he set about to convert Villiers from a potential enemy into an actual friend and supporter. "You are now the King's favorite," he told him, "so voted and so esteemed by all."

"Your office is vague, but your power is enormous. And whatever you might think to the contrary, you are by no means free from responsibility. For, in the eyes of the world, you're nothing less than a buffer, interposed between the people and their prince." "If the King commits an error and is loath to avow it, or if you commit the fault, or have willingly permitted it, you may perhaps be offered as a sacrifice to appease the multitude." Therefore, he went on, you should organize and administer this vague office of yours as efficiently, if not more so, than any of the regular offices of government. Concretely, he suggested that Villiers set up a panel of referees or experts "whom you think you can trust."

Each of these experts should be well versed in his own speciality, and the specialities should be religion, law, home affairs, foreign affairs, war by sea-or-land, trade, and the King's household. When petitions were received in his office, Villiers should have them copied and sent to the cognizant expert, or experts. Nor should he make any decision on them until his experts had had 20 days to study them and had written their opinions on them for or against.

Where Villiers would have charge of the executive branch of the new government, the prophetic Bacon would have charge of policy planning. As he had told the King, "I hope by my care the inventive power of the [Privy] Council will be strengthened, who commonly do exercise rather their judgments than their inventions." However, here too, Villiers could play an important role. For if the best policies were to prevail, the privy Council should have complete "freedom of discourse and determination." And it was Villiers' responsibility to keep the King from "overpowering the board too much" and from rash and ill-considered decisions of his own.

"You are bound to be his monitor, not in a saucy way which may not take with him, but at seasonable times which you may, nay, you must, watch for. An admonition from a dead author or a caveat from an impartial pen," he suggested, will work far better than "downright advice." But, at the same time, "you must always stand upon your watch to give him true intelligence. If you flatter him, you betray him. If you conceal the truth of those things from him which concerns his justice or his honor (although not the safety of his person), you are as dangerous a traitor to his state as he that riseth in arms against him. A false friend is more dangerous than an open enemy."

No doubt Villiers was very much on his good behaviour during his first months as favorite. He was only 24, with no University training and no experience in government save as Gentleman of the Bedchamber and as private companion to Prince Charles, the Prince of Wales. Yet, blind as Bacon always was to the limitations of his "instruments for doing good to the state," he could not have been totally blind. And very early he must have known that where Somerset's weakness lay in his passions, Villiers' lay in his excessive family loyalty.

His ambitious mother, now Lady Compton by a third marriage, had started life as a chambermaid in the home of Sir George Villiers, his father. She had married her employer, and then two other gentlemen in succession. When her son became the King's favorite, she saw to it that she and all her kinfolk were brought to court. Her daughters and female relations she had polished up with French instructors and then married to earls or their eldest sons. Her sons and male relations, after similar instruction, were married to countesses. Even her servants, her midwives, and cooks, had to be elevated; according to one report, she had them wedded to knights. Having enriched her family's blood, she then proceeded to enrich its fortunes. Though the typical Villiers, according to one gossip, "could scarce hold the rank of a Justice of the Peace," she had them all assigned to important or lucrative posts in the government. Meanwhile, they had taken over the best suite in the palace. When their marriages proved fruitful, as one gossip put it, "little children ran up and down the King's like rabbit starters about their boroughs."

In the ensuing years, Lady Compton would prove too much for Bacon in the struggle for the favorite's mind. But in these early days, at least, Bacon managed to hold his own. A few months after Villiers had first tentatively agreed to Bacon's plan, he suggested that Bacon should pay him a fee in return for his pressing Bacon's suit for Lord Chancellor. Other courtiers were willing to pay him for this office, he said, one of them as much as £50,000. Why, then, should Bacon get it for nothing? But Bacon reminded him that such jobbery was inconsistent with the new regime in which Villiers might make such a great name for himself. It would do you no good, he suggested, that "worthless persons should make a note that I get nothing [for my reforms] but pains, and enemies, and a little popular reputation."

Suppose Bacon sold the office of the Attorney General as Villiers would sell the office of the Lord Chancellor. "I could have more profit than I desire, and could oblige all the world and offend none; which is a brave condition for a man's private. But my heart is not on these things." Nor should Villiers' heart be on these things either. "If you would put your strength to this business," he concluded, "I know it is done. And that done, many [fine] things more will begin." Being still uncertain of his own position and feeling, perhaps, that Bacon's counsel and reputation were worth more than the fees of the other candidates, Villiers took this rebuff gracefully. From this time on, at any rate, and until Bacon's promotion was officially confirmed, he worked for him, more or less on Bacon's own terms.

CHAPTER SIX

200 DAYS ON THE THRONE

"It is a strange desire to seek power and to lose liberty; or to seek power over others and to lose power over a man's self."

—*Bacon, "Of Great Place"*

On May 7, 1617, Bacon was formally inducted as Lord Keeper of the Privy Seal, the same office as that of the Lord Chancellor, but with a lesser title, and with the understanding that the greater title would be his on good behaviour. At this point, Bacon would have done well to abandon his plans for a perfect monarchy and devote all his idealism to the research college, which he had been quietly building ever since his taking office. Twice now, he had tried to get King James' court operating the way he thought it should, and twice he had failed. If he failed again in this conspicuous office, he might very well lose all the prestige that he had won, if not the office itself.

It was remarkable enough, he wrote later, that he, "a man born for letters rather than anything else, and compelled by a certain fatality into active [political] life, should be raised by a prudent King to the greatest posts of honor, trust and employ." Yet he owed it to the King, he thought, to make a third attempt. And once again, in an excess of self-confidence, he celebrated his promotion as though all his magnificent dreams were now about to come true.

In point of "bravery and multitude of servants," one courtier said, this induction surpassed any staged by any of his predecessors; those who recalled his "humble beginnings" were "frankly amazed." The King himself was not there, nor was Villiers, now the Earl of Buckingham. They had gone off on a tour of Scotland with a large entourage of their own. But inevitably, this added all the more lustre to the occasion, for in the King's absence, Bacon would be Lord Lieutenant of the Realm, or acting King.

His induction proper was preceded by a parade from Gray's Inn on the northern boundary of London to the Great Hall in Westminster. According to one report, it numbered more than two hundred horsemen, arranged in rank according to the established rules of precedence. Besides his own private retinue, which now numbered about one hundred gentlemen, he was accompanied by the Queen's retinue, the Prince of Wales' retinue, the Lords of the Council, the Judges, the members of the Inns of Court, and finally "all the knights and gentlemen that could get horses and footclothes." No doubt he would have wished for a more complete representation of the latter group, for it was inconceivable to him that his new government could take effect without them. However, following the dissolution of the last Parliament, the King had ordered home all gentlemen not having business with the court. Rather ungraciously, James had told them: "Here at London, gentlemen, you are like ships in a sea which show like nothing. But in your country villages, you are like ships in a river which look like great things."

Arrived at the Great Hall, the order of precedence was reversed. The gentlemen and courtiers of the lower rank filled in, then the Lords of the Council, and finally behind his servants bearing the mace and the Great Seal of the new Lord Keeper. At his approach all removed their hats, and when he stood finally before his judicial chair, they took their seats. Gravely and with great dignity he then related what "His Majesty had charged me with when he gave me the Seal," "and what rules I had taken for the fulfillment of his commandments." He had taken great pains with this speech. Someone told him later that "not these seven years was there such a preparation."

However, to the chagrin of many informants and letterwriters, he would not permit a copy of it to be distributed until he had brought it to a high polish and until the King's own copy had been dispatched. In the speech he said nothing specifically about his long-range plans. But by hints here and there, he successfully created the impression that they were all about to be

launched into a "New World." His speech ended, he asked the assembly to
stay and hear a motion by a young lawyer, the brother of the Earl of Huntington, and as the young man came forward, he sat back in his chair.

"The rising unto place is laborious," he had written in the *Essays*. "By
pains men come to greater pains, and it is sometimes base, and by indignities men come to dignities." The compromise by which he had arrived
at his present dignity had undoubtedly left their mark on him. At 56, his
face was deeply lined, his hair was grey, and he was half crippled with gout.
Theoretically, these compromises should not have affected him at all. His
noble purposes, he believed, exempted him from the rules of ordinary mo-
rality. Yet in his prayers to God Almighty, he later confessed that "ever as
my worldly blessings were exalted, so secret darts from Thee have pierced
me. And when I have ascended before men, I have descended in humiliation
before Thee."

It was during an attack of these "secret darts" perhaps, that he was suddenly recalled to the Great Hall. The young lawyer did not know how to
proceed "being as his friends said, not provided, but called on the sudden."
Nor, under the circumstances, did Bacon know how to prompt him. He
too, began to falter and to reach for words as on his first gauche appearance
before the House of Commons 24 years before. This weakness did not last
long. But by the time he had got control over himself and the young man,
everybody wondered whether a man of "so tender a constitution both of
body and mind" would be "able to undergo the burden of so much business
as his place requires."

For a time Bacon also shared these doubts. That night he did not rest
well, and the next day in reporting the ceremony to Buckingham, he noted:
"Yesterday I took my place in Chancery. There was much ado and a great
deal of world. But this matter of pomp, which is heaven to some men, is
hell to me, or purgatory at least." Later, when Count Gondomar, the Spanish Ambassador, called at the palace to congratulate him, Bacon told him:
"I thank God and the King for this honor, but yet if I could be rid of the
burden, I would very willingly forbear the honor." Then he told Gondomar
that as soon as he had put the court on a reform basis, as the King had directed him to do, he would retire to his research college at Gorhambury.
Gondomar was so skeptical about this that, in reply, he told Bacon of an
old Spanish fable. According to this fable, the only rats that talk of retiring

are those that have quietly laid up a large hoard of Parmesan cheese. Bacon smiled sardonically, later including this conversation in his collection of witticisms. Yet Gondomar's skepticism about his high purpose and great designs was shared by almost all the courtiers, and this was a much more serious matter than Bacon realized.

In the next few days he recovered both his physical strength and moral courage. Now to confound his critics and to show them that he would expect nothing from them that he would not give himself, he turned in one of his most amazing performances. Prior to his induction as Lord Keeper (he had received the Great Seal on March 7) he had missed "2 Star Chamber days out of 3" and the meetings of the Privy Council repeatedly had to be postponed because of his absences. Now he "took pains more like the beast with 4 legs than like a man with 2 legs."

His gout still troubled him, but by sheer force of concentration he put it out of his mind. "I have been a little imperfect in my foot," he told Buckingham. "If this be gout," which he would "neither acknowledge nor much disclaim," it is a "good natured gout" and believed it was probably induced by the change from the "field air" of Gray's Inn to the "Thames air" of Whitehall. By June 6, one month after his induction, he reported proudly that he had finally "made even with the business of the kingdom for common justice. Not one cause unheard. The lawyers drawn dry of all the motions they were to make. Not one petition unanswered. And this I think could not be said in our age before." Admittedly, his health was worse than ever. But it was worth it. "The duties of life are more than life. And if I die now, I shall die before the world be weary of me, which in our times is somewhat rare."

Having set a high standard in his own bailiwick, he now set about to do likewise for the rest of the court. At a banquet for the judges, held in a "private withdrawing chamber," he painted a pen portrait of the perfect judge—a sound scholar, a good and sound administrator, a loyal subject, a humble and essentially decent man. Swearing in the new Baron of the Exchequer, he advised him that if he took the trouble to make a truly accurate inventory of the King's taxable property instead of following the slipshod method of his predecessors, he would save the people "much trouble and vexation" and yield "much profit" to the Crown. The same day, he advised a new councillor of Ireland to dedicate himself to the art of civilizing backward nations. Ireland will double her wealth and population within the next seven years, he predicted confidently. Therefore, "you must set it down with yourself to be not only a just governor" ("as if it were in England"), but under the King and the Deputy "you are to be a master builder and a master planter [colonizer]." For many years Bacon had urged the King to have "the daily acts of the palace" recorded in official journals. This was the practice of the "ancients," he said. To start the ball rolling on this reform, he would soon appoint "some grave and sound lawyers with some honorable stipend to be reporters of all cases" in his Court of Chancery.

Now the shoe was on the other foot. Instead of fearing that he was too weak to go through with his duties, his opponents (who comprised the great majority of the courtiers) feared that he was too strong. If Bacon kept on with his plans for the perfect monarchy, clearly they would have to learn their duties all over again. And since his actions were otherwise unimpeachable, they professed to believe that he was trying to usurp the throne—the actual throne of England, that is, not the throne of nature which was, of course, his real object. The leader of this faction was Sir Ralph Winwood. He was the Secretary of State, the second highest officer of the court and Bacon's immediate inferior. In a letter full of highly exaggerated charges, he urged the King to return at once and restore the status quo. To emphasize the danger, he said that the Lord Keeper had taken residence in the King's lodgings, had made all the councillors attend his motions, and had received ambassadors and other dignitaries in the Banqueting House as though he were actually King. But James, it seems, was more amused than distressed by this tale. Contrary to his usual practice, which was to read his letters privately with Buckingham, he read this one aloud to all his followers, and apparently, they too, saw the absurdity of it. In his reply, he told Winwood, that so far as he could see, the Lord Keeper was acting well within his instructions.

Winwood, however, was not to be put off. Rebuffed on this score, he began actively to plot the recall of Sir Edward Coke, the former Lord Chief Justice and Bacon's lifelong enemy. This was a very shrewd manoeuver. Bacon had played a part in Coke's downfall less than a year before. Rightly or wrongly Bacon had always regarded Coke as a major stumbling block in the unfolding of his great design. So when Coke was brought before the King for having exceeded his authority in a case involving the royal prerogative, Bacon had willingly argued against him. However, Coke had gone down

with a magnificent show of courage. While all his inferior judges had grov-
elled "on all fours," Coke had stood on his own two feet and defended his
position. "When the case shall happen," he had said, "I shall do that which
shall be fit for a judge to do." For this defiance, he was stripped of all his
offices.

About six months later, however, he had indicated his desire to be restored to "royal favor," "without which he could no longer breathe," and
had "acknowledged with much sorrow his former respectless behaviour."
Buckingham had encouraged him. Coke, he said, might be restored to the
Privy Council, though not to his judgeship, if he would marry his 14-year-
old daughter, Frances, to Buckingham's brother, Sir John Villiers, and settle
upon her a dowry of about £10,000. Coke was willing enough to buy his
way back into the King's favor, but not on Buckingham's terms. Thus, the
negotiations had been broken off. Then, quietly, Winwood entered the
scene as Buckingham's ally. So skillfully did he manage Coke that by June
of this year he had got him to agree, not merely to Buckingham's original
figure, but to another £20,000 in addition.

Of this plot, Bacon knew surprisingly little, and what he knew of it, he
could not take seriously. His mind was wholly preoccupied with his great
schemes. Having completed all the reforms that the King had authorized
him to make, and perhaps a few more, he now made his preparations for
launching his research college "as his Majesty shall know by the grace of
God at his return." Winwood had not concealed his hostility to the Lord
Keeper and his utopian schemes. One day at the council board, there was a
tiff. Winwood gave a hearty kick to the Lord Keeper's dog which had curled
up on his seat. Bacon admonished him for his cruelty, saying, "But every
gentleman doth love a dog." But later, when the Queen asked him why the
Secretary of State had taken such a strong dislike to him, he could give no
plausible explanation of it. "Madam, I can say no more but that he is proud
and I am proud." If worse came to worst, if Winwood should bring his opposition to a head, Bacon, oddly enough, still believed he could count on
the King's and Buckingham's support. All his actions he reported directly to
the royal pair in Scotland. One of his friends who was close to them had just
assured him that "your courses are such as you need not fear to give copies
of them."

In those days of violent individualism, however, no plot, whether large or small, was ever managed without some shattering explosion, revealing all. In this case, Winwood had failed to give due consideration to Coke's beserker wife, Lady Hatton. Lady Hatton was eager enough for her husband's restoration: in the last hours before Coke's downfall, she had pleaded for him at the council table. But she was also apparently something of a feminist, for after 20 years of married life with Coke, she still kept the name of her first husband who had left her so much property, and she still pointedly maintained her own household separate from Coke's. Lately, Winwood had managed to get her to live with Coke again. But he had not told her about the secret plans for the proposed marriage between her daughter and Sir John Villiers.

When she found out about these plans, she seized her daughter and took refuge "first in Lady Withipole's house in the country, and thence privily to a house of the Lord of Argyle's at Hampton Court." Coke, who was equally adept at this kind of thing, followed closely on her heels. Winwood had armed him with a warrant for the child's recovery. This Lady Hatton ignored. With an improvised battering ram, Coke then "brake open diverse doors" of Argyle's house, seized his daughter from her mother's arms, and made off with her. Lady Hatton gathered a small army, comprised of "Lord Houghton, Sir Edward Sackville, Sir Robert Rich and others, with three score of men and pistols" and gave chase. Luckily, her coach was "overturned" or "tired in the pursuit after him" (the account differed), and "they met not." If they had, there "was like to be strange tragedies." For Buckingham's mother was in Coke's coach, as was Clem, Coke's fighting son. "And they all swore they would die in the place before they would part with [the child]."

That afternoon the Lord Keeper was napping in his temporary quarters at Dorset House (his permanent quarters at York House, his birthplace, were being remodeled for him) when he was awakened by a woman's hysterical scream. The Papists had risen again, he thought, or the apprentices of London, for these possibilities, we know, were never far from his thoughts. Greatly alarmed, he called his servants, who came running to his bedstead with pikes and halberds in readiness. But to his astonishment, there in the midst of them stood the distraught Lady Hatton.

"Pray, my Lord," she said, admitting responsibility for the shriek, "I am but a cow which hath lost her calf." But the Lord Keeper still didn't know what she was talking about. Turning to the doorkeeper, he asked how this woman had been admitted to his chambers.

"I warned my Lady Hatton," he replied, "that your Lordship was not to be disturbed. But she inveigled me to let her stay in the next room where my Lord lay that she might be the first to speak with you after you were stirring. But as soon as she was alone, she rose up and bounced against my Lord's door." It must be mentioned that Lady Hatton had good reason for this breach of propriety. Prior to her engagement to Coke 20 years before, Bacon had courted her. Now, but for the grace of God, this violent woman might have been his wife instead of the less violent Lady Alice.

At any rate, after listening to Lady Hatton's tale, Bacon realized for the first time how seriously this silly squabble endangered his own regime. He saw not that it constituted "a riot and disturbance such as hath not happened since His Majesty's departure into Scotland" and that it was his duty to settle it at once. Summoning the Privy Council in emergency session, he told them what Lady Hatton had told him, that her daughter was in a state of shock "by occasion of the fright she has taken." At his suggestion, Coke and Lady Hatton with their respective private armies were asked "to forbear all occasion of violence or disturbance whatsoever, as well as touching the person of their daughter or any other matter concerning that business." To make doubly sure about this, and also to ensure that the girl would have "proper physic and attendance" Coke was ordered to turn her over to the custody of the clerk of the Council. At the same time, Coke was ordered to appear before the Council in person and explain his actions.

But the belligerent Coke was no more impressed with Bacon's supposedly perfect government than he had been earlier with King James' tyranny. Some time before, he had kept the King's messengers waiting three hours until he had finished his night's sleep. "If he be disturbed in his sleep," his son Clem had explained, "he will not be fit for any business." On this occasion, Coke kept the Council waiting many days before complying with their orders. When he did finally make his appearance, Bacon told him that his lawlessness was inconsistent with the new order of things and would not be tolerated. When Coke tried to justify the housebreaking on legal grounds, Bacon might have thrown back at Coke the admonition that Coke had once used against him, that "You should draw your learning out of your law books, not out of your brains." In any event, there was nothing in those books, Bacon said, that entitled a former Chief Justice to take the law into his own hands. On the contrary, a "man of his quality" should set the example. After this slating, the Privy Council agreed with him that the case should be turned over to the Star Chamber for a formal trial.

Now Bacon turned his attention to Winwood, the real author of the disturbance. No doubt, he had been hard on Coke. But with Winwood, he got so heated that he went completely out of character. Anger, he used to say, was a "kind of baseness, as it appears well in the weakness of those subjects in whom it reigns." The true reformer should look upon his enemies with "pity and compassion." The scene of this explosion was the council board; the time, a few days after Coke's appearance. Among those present was Buckingham's mother, Lady Compton.

In the absence of the King, Bacon told them, he had been charged with the management of the King's affairs. This task he would perform to the best of his ability. But it was obviously difficult, if not impossible, so long as Winwood attempted to set the house on fire, even if "it were but to roast an egg." Winwood, he went on, was not acting in the general good, but merely for the sake of faction. "He is setting bias upon his bowl to the overthrow of his master's great and important affairs." Then turning to Lady Compton, he told her that he wished her well and her sons too. Other things being equal, he would have no objection to the marriage of Sir John with Coke's daughter. But in the present instance, she had simply allowed herself to be duped into a plot for "weakening and distracting the King's service."

Throughout this tirade, Winwood sat silent, but composed. For one thing, as has been said before, he had no sympathy for Bacon's idealistic regime. For another thing, he now had the means of putting an end to them. For, unbeknownst to Bacon, the King had already given his consent to the marriage treaty in all its details, including the restoration of Coke to the Privy Council. When it was his turn to speak, at last, he assumed an air of injured innocence. He had been "too much trampled on with ill language," he said. There are many ways of serving the King, and his own was just as good as that "of the greatest of this board." Dramatically, then, he produced the letter from James, which showed that Bacon's disposition of this affair ran exactly contrary to His Majesty's wishes. By this letter, indeed, it would seem that it was Bacon and not Winwood who was setting the house on fire.

This was a stunning blow to the embattled Lord Keeper. Not only did it affect this particular matter of the Coke case, but conceivably it might also constitute a renunciation of his whole program. Obviously, there had been some gross misunderstanding, either on the part of Buckingham or the King, or both. Resuming his quiet, statesmanlike air, he wrote to the King, asking that he reconsider his decision in the light of these larger implications: "Your state is at this time not only in good quiet and obedience, but in good affection and disposition. Your judges are in good temper. Your justices of peace, which is the body of the gentlemen of England, grow to be loving. All mutinous spirits grow to be a little poor, and to draw in their horns." (In view of the existing ruckus, this last statement was palpably untrue. With more justice, Bacon might have said that at his suggestion a reclamation project "for the improvement and recovering of grounds from the desert to the garden" had been or soon would be made, and likewise, a geographical project for the survey of the "seawalls or poemerium of your island.")

"Again your Majesty may have perceived that as far it was fit for me to advise, I was ever for the present occasion. But this, my advice, was ever conditional that your Majesty should go to a Parliament with a council united and not distracted." With Coke restored, this would be manifestly impossible. "He is by nature unsociable, and by habit popular and too old now to take a new ply." Above all, he is lawless. "If he raiseth such a smoke to get in, [men can only] conclude that he will set all on fire when he is in."

To this lofty but somewhat inflated review of his achievements, the Lord Keeper received no coherent reply, but rather a barrage of cryptic letters that came sizzling across the Scottish border every week or so. During his tirade against Winwood at the council table, Bacon had suggested that Buckingham was a fickle youngster who had allowed his head to be turned by his sudden gush of fortune. "I must needs see further than his Lordship can" he had said, for "the height of his fortune hath made him too secure." This statement had been relayed by Winwood to the King and favorite, and this now stuck in their craw as his supreme offense. On hearing of it, Buckingham rhetorically turned his back to the Lord Keeper.

"I understand from London from some of my friends that you carried yourself with much scorn and neglect both towards myself and friends. Which if it prove true, I blame not you but myself who was ever your Lordship's most assured friend." The King, on the other hand, took up the statement and analyzed it at length. Secure, indeed!

"For our part we find [Buckingham] furthest from that vice of any courtier that ever we had so near about us." "Bacon must be jealous" of the youngster's judgment, more jealous, in fact, "than he ever deserved at your or any man's hands."

"I had rather go against Buckingham's mind than his good," Bacon said. Moreover, in making the remark, he had not meant to cause offense; he was merely stating a scientific fact.

"This is a judgment that the best authors make of the best and best tempered spirits."

To this the King had no reply except to say sardonically, "You have answered yourself."

Whatever this cryptic comment meant for the Lord Keeper's future (and certainly it didn't look good), one thing was clear: that Bacon had failed to get the King to reverse himself on the Coke case. The indictment against the former Chief Justice was withdrawn; the Star Chamber proceeding was cancelled; and young Frances Coke was returned to her father. With this retreat, moreover, Bacon's perfect monarchy vanished as though it had never existed at all save in his own mind, and his enemies were openly exultant. Buckingham's mother went about the court like a black witch "who could do hurt, but no good," speaking of Bacon with "some bitterness."

Winwood sharpened his knife for his final hour of vengeance. "As the Lord Keeper's tongue hath been a razor to me," he told his friends, "so shall mine be to him." Indeed, in all the antechambers of the palace, courtiers buzzed with "innumerable, malicious and detracting speeches."

As Buckingham told Bacon after their reconciliation, they were like "dogs that love to set upon him that they see once snatched at." Indeed, one of them went so far as to send Buckingham a formal petition of grievances against the regime "as if no music were more pleasing to my ears than to rail of you."

Throughout this trying period, Bacon, as usual, maintained his confidence in ultimate victory. "Your Majesty's letters," he told the King, "have grieved me more than any event in my life." Yet after carefully reading them over again, he had also taken comfort from them. For "intermixed" with the many royal rebukes (including a pointed reference to him as plain "Mr. Bacon") were also "passages of trust and grace." So when the King started his trip home, Bacon sent Yelverton, his loyal Attorney General, to meet the royal party halfway and to find out just where he stood. 80 miles north of London, at Daventry, the two parties met. The interview, like the King's letters, was neither wholly depressing, nor wholly encouraging.

"I have with much joy seen the face of my master, the King," Yelverton reported, "though more clouded towards me (and you) than I looked for." As to Buckingham, his mind was obviously poisoned and "mislead" by the "misformation" supplied by the Winwood faction. However, he had assured Yelverton that he would not "secretly bite" Bacon, but would "openly oppose him to his face." Thus, Yelverton went on, if Bacon would meet the royal party at Woodstock, their next resting place, just north of London, he might turn the tables on his enemies and bring the favorite back into camp.

"You must open yourself bravely and confidently," he went on. You "must not seem dismayed" in the slightest. Above all, you must not "single yourself from the other Lords" of the Council; you must make them all share the blame with you. This, he admitted, was a difficult feat. But for a man of Bacon's finesse, a man "excelling all subjects in the art [science] of dissimulation," it was not impossible.

In short, Yelverton would have Bacon abandon his lofty defence and return to the battle on the same level as his opponents. At first, Bacon was inclined to agree. According to the rules of palace politics, in a misunderstanding of this kind, one must "entertain and amuse the party with some [diversionary] discourse" and "break the ice with words of less weight." A few days before, one Baynton, a disappointed office seeker, was heard on two occasions to have threatened the life of the King. The case had been referred by Yelverton to Bacon. So he, in turn, could legitimately take it up with the King. Moreover, it was urgent, "being upon the tenderest point of all"—namely, the King's safety.

Yet, on second thought, he decided that the case was so flimsy and immaterial that even James would see through it. After all, the man had not been "apprehended." According to the report, he was either an alcoholic or a lunatic, and there was even some question about his name—whether it was Baynton, or Baynam, or what. Before he could think of some better approach, however, Bacon was seized by a despondency from which even Yelverton's encouraging words could not relieve him. What, he asked himself, was to be gained by affecting "bold discourse" and a confident air? Keeping himself in office as Lord Keeper? Perhaps. But his perfect monarchy had vanished into thin air, and barring some new and unforeseen crisis, there was no chance that it would be brought back to life again.

From the very beginning, it had been palpably absurd that he could persuade this court singlehandedly to adopt his visionary reforms. Even now, we have yet to see a government as perfect as the one called for in Bacon's blueprints—a government completely dedicated "to the great and important affairs" of state and completely clear of "small wares and petty points of cunning." Yet, for a brief moment, he had given the world an impression of such a government, and his prophetic work was by no means finished. There was still the research project at Gorhambury.

With men and money now at his disposal, there was no reason why he could not bring this enterprise to fruition "in works of power and utility." How many such works he could actually bring forth, or whether the King in his present frame of mind, could effectively employ such works for the "betterment of man's bread and wine," he did not know. But whatever his doubts on these points, he would have to execute his plans, if for no other reason than to give the world "some [further] evidence of his honest mind and inclination towards the human race."

For the success of this enterprise, it was, of course, absolutely essential that he stay in office as Lord Keeper. Thus, he steeled himself to endure whatever humiliations the favorite might have in store for him. This is what he called "submission to the occasion and not to the man." Instead of boldly meeting the royal party at Woodstock, as Yelverton had advised him to do, he simply waited until they had returned to the palace and there, without cavil, defence, or argument of any kind, he humbly offered his "submission." According to a palace gossip, they put him in a room for lackeys and trencher-scrappers (dishwashers). For two days he sat there on an old wooden chest with his purse and his seal in his hand; when Buckingham finally received him, he fell "to his knees."

This story has been discredited. But whatever Bacon did or said, the Earl was so touched by it that, in his own words, he was transformed from "the person of a party into [that of] a peacemaker." In his turn, then, Buckingham went down on his knees before the King and asked that he, too, join in forgiveness for the erring Lord Keeper. It was not easy. The King was still inflamed by Bacon's successive acts and words of defiance. As the Earl later told him, "I dare say no other person would have been patiently heard in this suit but myself." The King, it seems, had planned to put some "public exemplary mark" on the Lord Keeper. But by the favorite's influence, he was persuaded to settle for something less—namely, "a kingly reprimand of so many councillors as were actors in this business," but without passion and "without accusing any particular persons by name."

About a month later, a great feast of reconciliation was held in Lady Hatton's palace. But save for the jubilant King and the favorite, it seemed more like a funeral than a festive occasion. Winwood had died suddenly the day before, possibly from the shock of seeing the Lord Keeper's return to favor. Coke returned to the Privy Council, only to discover that he too had been duped by Buckingham; in his chagrin and disappointment, he did not attend the feast either.

As to Bacon, a great transformation had come over him. Ostensibly, he was the life of the party. Every quarter hour he rose to toast "My Lady Elizabeth Hatton." This toast was seconded by the King, "and then by all the lords and ladies with great gravity and respect, and then by all the gallants in the next room." But to anybody who knew him well and who looked into his weary eyes, it was clear that his soul had left his body again for another long voyage through space and time. At a Lord Mayor's dinner, he "sat still and picked a little upon one dish only"; upon his return to York House, he could not explain his lack of appetite save to say that the food was "too light and dissipable" for him. When all the rest of the "great persons" were in the tilt yard, he would wander down to the Thames and talk with the fishermen about their catch. "Hope is a good breakfast," he told them dejectedly, "but a bad supper."

Even when he was confirmed in his office with the full title of Lord Chancellor on New Years day, 1618, he could not take any real interest in the life of the court. Of all the high officers, only three were aware of his plans for the launching of his research college and of his long preparation for this event. These were two privy councillors (the Earl of Arundel and Sir Julius Caesar), and one bishop (Archbishop Andrewes). It is doubtful that even they understood the enormous significance of these plans for mankind as a whole.

CHAPTER SEVEN

UNVEILING THE NEW MACHINE

"If any one shall call on me for works [inventions], I shall
tell him frankly without any imposture at all, that I hold it
enough to have constructed the machine, though I may not
succeed in making it work."

—*Bacon, "Proem," 1603*

Following the debacle of his two hundred days on the throne, Bacon,
now England's Lord Chancellor, spent every spare hour both on week-
ends and during vacations at his research college in Gorhambury. In his
original plans for this enterprise back in 1608, it had been his intention "not
merely to survey the new regions [of nature], like an auger taking auspices,
but to enter them like a general who means to take possession." But after 13
years of research, he had made no invention nor any discovery of any real
importance. And now at last he would admit that his original intention was
"a thing above my strength and beyond my hopes."

Nobody today can be surprised at this terrible anticlimax. For as everybody knows now, it was simply not in the cards for one man, in one fell
swoop to invent "all things possible." At this new debacle, a less determined
man would have thrown up his hands in despair, freely acknowledge that
nature had deceived him and sought solace in his official duties as the Lord
Chancellor. Fortunately for us, however (the world had a vested interest in

the preservation of Bacon's delusion), the man was indestructible. Lifting the wraps off his enterprise for the first time, he said his failure was due not to any technical errors, but rather to the shortage of men and equipment at his disposal. If his disciples would build an even more elaborate research college on the same principles, he assured them that they could turn this colossal failure into a colossal success.

The ideal research college, Bacon had told Queen Elizabeth, would include a complete library, a complete technological museum, a chemical laboratory with mills and furnaces and a complete botanical garden, "wherein whatsoever plant the sun of diverse climates has brought forth, may be set and cherished." This garden would be "built about with rooms to stable in all rare beasts and to cage in all rare birds; with 2 lakes adjoining, the one of fresh water, the other of salt for like variety of fishes." Such an establishment, he had said, was beyond the means of any but a King, or a Pope. But out of his own earnings as a government official he had already constructed as much of it as he needed for demonstration purposes, and with further help from the King, could have completed the rest if it.

Somewhere on his Gorhambury estate he had an experimental orchard, stocked with "all manner of fruit trees that would grow in England." With it, or near it, was a "hot bed" or dung pile, which he used for seed testing, and a greenhouse where beet roots and radishes were grown in earthen pans and into which boughs of trees were brought for study. In much the same manner, he had an experimental fishery, stocked with as many different kinds of fish as the seamen of the Royal Navy could provide for him. Also he had just paid £300 for the installation of an aviary in York House, his new London palace, an aviary so rigged that "the birds may have scope and natural nesting and that no foulness appear on the floor." One day a giant crane escaped through one of the aviary windows. One can imagine the amusement of passers-by as a washerwoman, with her laundry spread over the palace steps, chased after it and later as the Lord Chancellor rewarded her for the return of a prized specimen.

These installations were set in the midst of royal splendor. Among other things, he had recovered "the desert" around the Gorhambury pondyards about a mile north of his father's manor and converted it into a showplace comparable to Prince Charles' place at nearby Berkhamsted. The ponds were enclosed with a brick wall and railings; the water was drained off, the bottoms were lined with fish mosaics made up of multi-colored stones, then the ponds were refilled again. Between the pondyards and the old manor house, a tremendous park was laid out with what looks like a three-lane highway. The middle lane was wide enough for three coaches running abreast, and the lanes themselves were lined with stately elms, oaks, chestnuts and beeches.

On either side of the park were woods, filled with bird sanctuaries, summer houses and shaded walks, while at either end of the parks were formal gardens after the fashion of the time. For entertaining his fellow officers of the court, he had constructed a Roman-style banqueting hall. This was set on an island in the middlemost pond and connected with the mainland by a bridge. It was a handsome structure, paved with white and black marble, covered with Cornish slate, "with Chimneys neatly cast and without too much glass."

After laying out the grounds, Bacon had built an administration building which he called Verulam House after the old Roman city of Verulamium, the ruins of which were less than a half mile off. Here, too, the emphasis was on the splendors of nature. On the roof of this house was a promenade overlooking the park. At the top of the broad stairwell he had installed a trick mirror so that when he entered his study, the whole room was illuminated with the reflection of the garden below. In his father's old manor, for much the same purpose, he had added a glass-enclosed portico, on one side of which were birds, beasts and flowers, painted over glass. These were the high spots. But there was not a nook or cranny in either house that was not brightened with colored lanterns or balls of colored glass, hardly a door that was not painted with a Greek or Roman god in gold hatching, and hardly a staircase whose posts were not studded with statues of monks, friars, and the like.

At first glance, it would seem that the magnificence of this college was out of all proportion to its few actual scientific installations. And certainly in this regard, it outshone all later establishments of the kind. Bacon's own explanation was that "in fame of learning the flight will be slow without some feathers of ostentation." Yet in the construction at Verulam House, his new headquarters, he also made several innovations that have a very modern ring to them.

The typical manor of the time, he argued, was beautiful like "the enchanted palaces of the poets" but was also uncomfortable. "Houses," he wrote, "are built to live in and not to look on." Air conditioning as such was, of course, beyond his range. Nonetheless, in building "this little pile" he took into account all its essential features. By proper location, he sought to avoid the dampness of many of the "fairest palaces." By cutting down the number of doors and windows, he sought "to prevent drafts which are a great enemy to health."

Improved temperature control was also one of his objects. For winter heating he had the chimney tunnels from all the fireplaces drawn into one main tunnel (an attempt at central heating), and seats installed around it. For better insulation against summer heat, he had (or planned to have) the windows on three sides completely walled up, thus providing "rooms from the sun, both for the forenoon and afternoon."

Perhaps his most ingenious innovation was his method of clearing the house of kitchen odors. He located the kitchen, the larder and the servant's quarters underground. In the old manor apparently, these were located "just below stairs." The "steam" of the kitchen had come up to him as "in a tunnel" and he had had to taste "the servants' dinner after his own." In the matter of temperature control, it should be added, Bacon's arrangements were not wholly successful. He could design a summer house (Verulam House) or a winter house (Gorhambury House), but he could not provide for both seasons in the same house.

Having got thus far with his research college, Bacon then began to speculate on all the great inventions he might have made if only he could have completed "the design." One can imagine him now, in his full glory as the imaginary conqueror of nature, sitting on one of the garden benches with his head cocked and resting on his arm, or riding in his coach down one of his highways after a spring shower and sniffing the air which he said was very wholesome at that time because it was filled with "nitre," the spirit of the universe, or dictating notes to William Rawley, his chaplain and chief secretary, while tramping on alleys of burnet, wild thyme and water mints, "which perfume the air being trodden upon and crushed." Returning to the house, his chaplain tells us, "he would fall to work again, and so suffer no moment to slip from him without improvement." Meanwhile, he had a harpist in the room adjoining his study, playing music that "feedeth the disposition of the spirits."

Bacon's agenda of inventions for his perfected college had now become grandiose—so grandiose, indeed, that even today, with a world-wide research organization, science had still not exhausted it. According to a memorandum that was found among his papers after his death (for fear of ridicule he did not publish it at this time) it consisted of some 24 items, including weather control (the artificial "raising of tempests"), the restitution of youth and the prolongation of life, the transmutation of metals, facial surgery ("the altering of complexions"), and the "drawing of new foods out of substances not now in use." In short order, he believed, his disciples would develop all the items on this agenda.

But his own ambition for this achievement died hard, and despite his public declarations to the contrary, he would never wholly give up the hope of beating his disciples to the punch. In some cases, he made fancy little working models of his proposed inventions. Unable to make a perpetual motion machine (nobody else has either), he had a statue of Neptune set up in the ponds, "neatly cut out in wood holding his trident in his hand and aiming with it at a duck which perpetually turned round with him and a spaniel swimming after." Another project that he was reluctant to leave to his disciples was "to raise fruits out of season" and "to make them greater and sweeter and of differing taste, smell, color and figure from their nature." It would be two hundred years before the American grape growers would make this dream a reality by developing the Concord grape. Yet here at Gorhambury, Bacon conducted certain preliminary experiments on it.

His reports on these experiments accurately forecast the spirit, if not the style, of the reports of our Department of Agriculture experimental stations. In one such experiment, for example, he tried to find some fertilizer that would grow wheat faster than the conventional horse manure. He tried cow manure, pigeon manure, human urine, 3 kinds of wine, and 3 artificial "composts," namely, solutions of chalk, basalt and soot. Scientifically he kept tabs on how the "composts" were put together. Also he grew one culture as a control without fertilizer. The results were not startling. None of his "composts" worked any better than horse manure, and some of them worked so badly that they killed the wheat. However, the experiment had been worth trying, and others like it should be attempted. For "fertilizers are cheap things, and the acceleration of growth is a matter of gain, if the goodness of the crop answer the earlyness of the coming up, as it is like it will."

In another experiment, he tried to find a wrapping that would ripen green apples. The theory was that the wrapping would bring forth the "spirits of the body." Here is Bacon's own account of the experiment: "There were taken green apples and laid in straw; in hay; in flour; in chalk; in lime; covered with crabs; closed up in wax; shut in a box. There was also an apple hanged up in smoke. After a month, the apple in wax was as green and fresh as before; in smoke, turned old and mellow; in lime, well-matured.

"Note that the taste of these apples (in lime) was good, and therefore it is the experiment fittest for use. . . . The apples covered with crabs and onions were likewise well matured. The cause not any heat, but for that crabs and onions draw forth the spirits of the apple and spread them equally through the body." As compared with the experiment mentioned above, this one was an outstanding success. For "when all of these [apples] were compared with another apple of the same kind that lay of itself, they were found to be more sweet and more yellow and also appeared to be more ripe." On the other hand, this experiment had far less significance than the other, being a mere "toy" in point of practical utility.

So much for his casual experiments. With a thousand men to help him, some of the items of this agenda could have been completed within his own lifetime, he believed, and the rest, within the next century. Here, again, Bacon was vastly underestimating the complexities of the enterprise. However, in justice to him, it must be added that he would have so organized his researchers that their work would have been vastly sped up.

"Men will only begin to know their own power," he wrote, "when each performs a separate part, instead of undertaking in crowds the same work." His scheme of organization, moreover, was suggestive of that employed more recently in the Manhattan District Project—the project that produced the atomic bomb.[13] It consisted of an administrative pyramid, rising from

---

13   The author refers to the approach taken in the Manhattan Project (which occurred only about a decade prior to his writing of this book), where multiple parts of the US were tasked with different objectives and processes for ultimately manufacturing atomic fission bombs.

the "miners" (experimenters) at the bottom through "compilers" (notetakers), "dowry men" (inventors), "lamps" (project directors), "inoculators" (special experimenters), and finally reaching its apex with the "interpreter of nature" (the chief administrator). Naturally this top job he would have reserved for himself.

But how his successor would have been chosen after his death he never made clear. As we have seen, the secret of longevity was one of the items on his agenda, and he may well have assumed that once this secret was known, he would live long enough for the completion of the whole enterprise. Yet, as the discoveries and inventions were made, he would not have hogged the credit. Any man anywhere in the organization who made a contribution would have his statue in a Hall of Fame, especially designed for the purpose. His statue would be cast in brass, marble, cedar, iron, silver, or gold, according to the importance of his discovery.

In the course of his rise to Lord Chancellor, Bacon had attracted about a hundred men into his service. He was a considerate and tolerant administrator, and many "young gentlemen of blood and quality" had come to him. Bacon employed them as clerks, recorders and officials in the Chancery. But he also, apparently, expected them to help him in the one research project which he deemed to be clearly within his compass—namely, the discovery of the law of heat.

This was not so easy. It was not only that they were utterly untrained for this kind of thing, but also that they carried with them a lot of medieval baggage, completely out of place at Gorhambury. The great majority, it may be supposed, like most of their contemporaries at court, were completely skeptical about the enterprise. They regarded it as slightly *infra dig* to muddy their hands. They would rather use Bacon's college for breeding fast racehorses than for growing fruits out of season. On the other hand, the few men who were genuinely interested in it were so carried away with its miraculous possibilities that they couldn't concentrate on the humdrum research jobs he assigned them.

Take the case of William Rawley. In 1616, Rawley had applied for admission to Bacon's service straight out of the Cambridge divinity school. After trying him out first as rector at Landbeach, Bacon had taken him on, officially as chaplain, and unofficially as private secretary. Rawley was perhaps the most devoted servant Bacon would ever have. With Bishop

Andrewes he was one of the most ardent of Bacon's ecclesiastical supporters. Accurately he foresaw that "howsoever [my Lord's] body is mortal, yet no doubt his memory and works will live, and will in all probability last as long as the world lasteth." Yet we are amazed to find that Rawley was something of an astrologer, and believed his master, like everybody else, was subject to the "doctrine of horoscopes, the calculation of nativities, and the horary reign of the planets."

"The moon had some principal place in the figure of his nativity," Rawley wrote. "For the moon was never in her passion [that is, in eclipse] but he was surprised with a sudden fit of fainting." True, Bacon did have fainting spells. But this, he told Rawley, was due to natural causes—to emotional fatigue, perhaps. There was no scientific basis whatsoever, he added, to "horoscopes, nativities and the horary reign of the planets." Yet, the next time the moon was in eclipse, Rawley expected Bacon to faint again.

Thomas Bushell was another case in point. When Bushell had first joined Bacon's service, he was a youngster still in his teens, wild and irresponsible. Bacon had taken a personal interest in him, had polished, disciplined, and educated him at his own expense. Now he entrusted him with a high place in his service. In the ceremonies of the court, Bushell walked immediately before his lord carrying the Great Seal. At Gorhambury, he seems to have been one of the "dowry men," charged with inventing and constructing instruments. Bushell had great confidence in Bacon's inventive powers. Not only did he believe in them himself, but he managed to get other people outside of Gorhambury to believe in them. And after Bacon's death, he would try to cash in on this belief.

During the course of his service Bushell had devised a bellows for ventilating mine shafts, a minor variation of the bellows then in common use. Later he would claim that he was the sole trustee of Bacon's mining secrets and that "the Lord Chancellor's [scientific] theory did light the first candle to this and all other mines, [gadgets] of like nature." This claim he "substantiated" with forged papers, carving out for himself a fabulous career as a mine speculator, raising considerable sums both from Parliament and from private investors. Only his old companions at Gorhambury knew what a liar and scoundrel he was. Whenever they received a prospectus from him, contemptuously they would nail it to their wainscoting after the fashion of nailing counterfeit coins to the counter and vermin to the stable door.

Bacon, of course, was well aware of the difficulty of converting his impulsive and volatile servants into reliable research men. Some time later, when Thomas Hobbes came to work for him, he told this youngster, soon to become a great philosopher in his own right, "that he was the best note-taker he had ever had."

"Many times when I read of [the other men's] notes," he went on, "I scarce understood what they wrote because they understood it not clearly themselves." Nonetheless, with the proper discipline, he said these men could be shed of their delusions ("idols of the mind"), and be empowered to make the "clear observations" and "sound conclusions" essential to research. Scientific know-how, he said, was inborn in a few abnormal men like himself and Hobbes. But it could also be expounded, wrapped up and packaged, and passed on to others not naturally scientific. Theoretically this was sound enough, and most modern research is organized on this principle. Nor can there be any doubt that his formulation of scientific method was a forward step. However, like his servants, he too was carried away by its miraculous possibilities; hence he was in no position to discipline them. Indeed, the more he lectured to them, the more he confused them. Thus, inevitably, his attempt to discover the laws of heat was as ill-fated as his other research projects.

By a strange coincidence, Bacon's own physician and the King's, Dr. William Harvey, was one of the greatest experimental scientists of all time. Harvey had no pretentious agenda, no staff of assistants, not even a laboratory. Most of his research was done at a slaughterhouse where animals were bled after being pole-axed. However, Harvey knew instinctively what Bacon only pretended to know, and in 1616, one year before Bacon's elevation to the Chancery, had come up with one of the monumental discoveries of medical science—the correct analysis of the circulation of the blood. There was no great mystery about this discovery. During the course of a lifelong study of the human heart, he had got a hunch about it. Thereafter he didn't rest until he had proved this hunch by an exhaustive series of experiments, first on dogs and fish, later on men with ligatures.

Rugged individualist that he was, Harvey was rather contemptuous of Bacon's elaborate but fruitless operations. About 30 years later, he told Aubrey, the biographer, that he "esteemed the Lord Chancellor Bacon much for his style and wit, but would not allow him to be a great [scientist]." "He writes [science] like a Lord Chancellor," Harvey went on derisively, "but I have cured him." Apparently Harvey had tried to explain to Bacon just how research would be conducted. At this, he recalled, Bacon's piercing hazel eyes turned cold and flinty, "like the eyes of a viper."

Yet, for the purpose that was now uppermost in his mind, namely, to get his disciples to build a college of their own, Bacon did not have to conduct a successful research operation. Ignoring his actual results, and calling on his prophetic powers, "none of them superstitious and yet not all natural," he came forth with a new theory of heat—a theory that was vague perhaps, but suggestive of a valid one developed by Count Rumford almost two hundred years later.

"I do not invest these inventions of mine [*sic*] with any majesty," he wrote. "However I have somewhat advanced (as I make bold to think) the matter I now treat of." And considering that "among my contemporaries, I have been most engaged in public business," that "I am not very strong in health (which causes a great loss of time)" and that I "was the first explorer of this course, following the guidance of none," that was no mean achievement. At any rate, with this as "the final fruit" of his enterprise, there was no reason why his disciples could not rapidly press on to the total conquest of nature. Let "all good men lay aside prejudice and join for the common good." If there was some error in his "discovery" it could be rooted out and supplanted by new truth. For this, he predicted, was the way his enterprise would grow—"not by arguments, but by experience and the results of experience." "Science is not an opinion to argue about, but a work to be done."

❃

This public appeal was incorporated in the *Novum Organum*, or the *New Machine*, published on October 12, 1620. But what chance was there that it would be more effective than his previous appeal in 1605? Other things being equal, not much. Most of his disciples, or potential disciples, were students at the Universities, and their professors were still as much opposed to research as ever. Not only did the latter continue to profess faith in the outmoded learning of the ancients, but they had lately taken steps to put nature itself beyond the pale of legitimate inquiry—the stars in the heavens, the flowers and trees of the earth, the fish in the sea.

Bacon, as Lord Chancellor, could study these things freely on his palatial

estate at Gorhambury, and in his imagination, at least, penetrate all their secrets. But let some humble scholar try to imitate the Lord Chancellor, and
the authorities would condemn and punish the man as a "turbulent and
revolutionary spirit." This was true, not only of the humble scholar, but also
of Bacon's great scientific contemporaries.

Only five years before, the professors in Italy had turned Galileo over to
the Papal Inquisition with the result that Galileo's works were now on the
Index, and Galileo himself temporarily silenced. Harvey, having completed
the experiments referred to above, would not publish them for another decade, "fearing lest I have mankind at large for my enemies—so much doth
custom and doctrine and respect for antiquity influence men." Even then,
the professors of the Royal College of Physicians heaped so much abuse on
Harvey, that, according to Aubrey, "he fell mightily in his practice and twas
believed by the vulgar that he was crackbrained."

Bacon, of course, knew exactly what he was up against. During his days
as an unsuccessful office-seeker, he had already fought and lost one battle
with the professors. So now he used all the power and prestige of his high office to see that his disciples would have an easier time of it than he did. On
one hand, the Lord Chancellor urged faculty dignitaries "to retain freedom
of thought, and not to suffer the talent which the ancients have deposited
with you to lie dead in a napkin." On the other hand, he attempted to organize a little group of his own disciples right under the professors' noses.
At every opportunity, he provided them with equipment, books, and every
Christmas he sent them hams and other gifts.

When the late merchant, Sutton, had left a large endowment for a
grammar school, Bacon had tried and failed to divert the funds to the great
Universities for chairs in the natural sciences. But in 1618, probably at his
suggestion, his friend, Sir Henry Savile, gave a handsome endowment for
chairs in geometry and astronomy at Oxford, "these studies being now almost wholly unknown and forgotten." Part of the endowment was used for
the installation of the latest equipment: "spheres, globes, astrolabes, maps
and the like."

Having planted his "seed" among the students, Bacon now exploded
a shocking blast of gunpowder directly in the professors' faces. He accused
them of "turning men's minds away from nature" and "of groveling before blind and confused idols." He advised them, for their own posthumous

reputations, to forget these follies and "to bend their whole might towards the advancement of the sciences." This indictment had been drafted and redrafted over a period of 11 years, and was now inserted as a preface to his book. He had worked on it "like a lioness licking her cubs, till she brings them to the strength of their limbs."

But at the last minute, as publication date approached, Bacon seems to have got cold feet and added still another preface disclaiming "any attempt to disturb the teaching that now prevails in the Universities." However, his precaution proved unnecessary. For some reason or other, the professors were completely awed by him. Perhaps, it was the high rank and reputation of the author who signed the book, not with his name but with his titles. Perhaps, it was the defiant dignity of the frontispiece, which showed a ship in full sail, passing through the gates of Hercules, out of the narrow academic seas into the unknown scientific ocean, and under it the prophecy "Many shall pass through these gates and the sciences shall be advanced." Whatever it was, the professors made no protest and received this or a subsequent volume with a great show of politeness "in a very full congregation both of the doctors and the masters."

Now with the opponents of research temporarily silenced, and with the secrets of Gorhambury published for all to read, Bacon's enterprise began slowly to win new converts. In the early days, these converts were most conspicuous among the rising generation at Oxford and Cambridge, where Bacon noted, his books were "well-tasted." Soon there was other evidence of his widening influence. On manors and rich country estates, little research colleges were constructed with revolving ducks, aviaries, and experimental gardens after the Gorhambury model. There all of Bacon's inconclusive experiments were tried over again, and many new ones besides. Also from time to time, informal meetings were held among the disciples to discuss their findings. Nothing could damp their enthusiasm for this enterprise.

After 1640, when the people rose up against James' son, Charles I, and London became a city of barracks, their meetings sometimes had to be conducted secretly, or, as they put it, the college became "invisible." Yet it was during this period, ironically, that the enterprise made its greatest strides, gaining converts both among the Puritan professors at Oxford and among the idle royalists in exile in France. At the Restoration, it included more than a hundred active partisans, most of them literary men like John Milton, one of Bacon's earliest converts, and John Evelyn, the diarist. Moreover, since the new King, James' grandson, Charles II, was himself one of these partisans, they were now in a position to build a full-scale research college of their own, bigger than Gorhambury, and they hoped, more productive. In 1662 Charles II recognized this college, known then and now as the Royal Society; he gave them a charter, a mace, and later some Crown lands for a regular meeting place.

This was the delayed response to Bacon's second public appeal, and this was the one tangible fruit of a career otherwise completely locked in a dream world. Had he lived to be 101, he would no doubt have presided over the early meetings of the Royal Society, as he did in spirit, and no doubt he would have told them of the great opportunity that lay before them. This same speech he had made to King James and others many times in his own lifetime. This, he would have said, is "the beginning of a better ordering of man's life and business by the help of sound and true contemplations . . . After this beginning and the wheel once set turning, men shall suck more truth out of Christian pens than hitherto they have done out of heathen."

Yet on second thought, perhaps it was better that Bacon did not live on into this new age. For when his disciples sat down to the serious business of scientific research and when true scientists like Boyle and Newton took over the organization from the literary dreamers, they found that his blueprints for the conquest of nature were unworkable. His scientific method, for example, was absurdly complicated, and his agenda of inventions utopian. A century would pass before the first scientific invention, the steam engine, would be forthcoming. Now three centuries later,[14] with worldwide research organizations in the field, we have still not exhausted his list. Indeed, the more one considers the cost and complexity of modern research, the more fantastic it seems that one man could ever have hoped to invent "all things possible." Yet modern scientists are also coming to recognize that had not Bacon believed so doggedly in this otherwise futile enterprise, their own mighty establishment might never have been born at all.

In his own time Bacon's errors were still largely unknown. Also by a curious coincidence, a miniature version of one item on his agenda, "an ark for

---

14   The actual time reference would be three and a half centuries later.

submarine navigation," was launched about the same time as the *New Machine*. Designed by a Dutch engineer, it was submerged in six feet of water, and then more or less successfully rowed down the Thames. In December 1620, Sir Henry Wotton, the English Ambassador at Vienna, sent Bacon a complete report on another prophetic gadget, Kepler's camera obscura, the prototype of the modern camera. In this optimistic atmosphere none of Bacon's pretensions as potential conqueror of nature seemed too extravagant, and for the first time he was taken at his own valuation.

Just what he had done to establish this claim was a matter of dispute. More cautious observers, following Bacon's own lead, thought that "by his own hand he had further moved those pillars of [learning] which by the rest of the world were supposed immovable." Others, encouraged by the irresponsible Bushell, went further, saying that in one great effort he had "conned all the mysteries of nature" and that like some great magician, he could now produce all the items on the agenda. Both of these estimates, of course, missed the mark. However, in this enterprise, as Bacon had said, failure is sometimes more desirable than success. And here, if ever, was a case in point. If nothing else, he had created a magnificent new dream castle in which his disciples might dwell, until stone by stone over the long centuries, they would, partially at least, bring it to life. Who, then, would begrudge him this brisk hour of triumph amid so many hours of struggle and disappointment?

On January 22, 1621, his 60th birthday was celebrated at York House. "All the wits who could honor a language or help [science]" were there. In an ode especially written for the occasion, Ben Jonson tells us, everything in that "ancient pile" smiled upon—the crackling fire, the wine, and the guests—Bacon stood smiling back at them "as if some mystery thou didst!" The Elizabethans, Jonson wrote later, had produced many great men comparable to those of the ancient world. He mentioned Bacon's father, Sir Nicholas Bacon, also Essex, Raleigh, Sir Henry Savile and Egerton, Bacon's predecessor as Lord Chamberlain. But "this Lord," he said, stood alone, unrivaled not only by the Elizabethans but standing far out in front of the "insolent Greeks and the haughty Romans."

This was only the beginning. Thanks, in part, to the zeal of Tobie Matthew, his overseas missionary, "his fame was greater and sounded louder in foreign parts abroad than at home." When his new book was read by the leading Europeans (and his earlier books were now being widely translated), some of them were so enthusiastic about it that they came to England personally to congratulate him. One eminent foreigner insisted on getting his lifesize portrait so that his countrymen might see him as well as read him. Marquis d'Effiat, later the French Ambassador, told him at their first meeting, "Your lordship has ever been to me like the angels of whom I have often heard and read about in books, but whom I have never seen."

To this Bacon replied, "Sir, the charity of others doth liken me to an angel, but my own infirmities tell me I am a man." Thus, once more, as in his hectic two hundred days as acting King, the court was turned topsy-turvy with Bacon once more threatening the preeminence of his King. But this time, the old tyrant did not object.

On the contrary, he assured Bacon that "you could not have made choice of a subject more befitting your place and your universal and methodical knowledge." Then, adding his compliments to the others, he raised him one step higher in the peerage (Bacon had been created Baron of Verulam in 1618), creating him Viscount St. Albans. Bacon received his new title "with all ceremonies of robes and coronets, whereas the rest received theirs by patent."

Outwardly, Bacon remained calm under his accolade. "I have received far more honor than I expected from so abstruse an argument," he told Bishop Andrewes. But inwardly, he was so dizzy that he was blind again to his limitations. Indeed, despite all his past failures in this connection, he told the King that if only he could get further help for his enterprise, "even in your Majesty's lifetime, many noble inventions may be discovered for man's use." "Caesar's star will ripen this work which is for the bettering of men's bread and wine." However, the King's attention was completely occupied by the political crisis then raging, and Bacon did not press the point. Simultaneously, with the publication of the *New Machine*, the King had issued the writs for a new Parliament.

Shortly afterwards, Bacon told him that "the prognostics [for this Parliament] are not as good as I expected." Yet in preparing for what would obviously be a very difficult occasion, the King consulted his Lord Chancellor more than any other councillor. Eagerly he awaited Bacon's papers and memoranda on the questions of the day. When they arrived in the throne room, he snatched them greedily out of Buckingham's hand. On this front, too, the sudden shift of his fortune made Bacon dizzy and blind to his limitations. Having established himself (partially at least) in his role as the "inventor of all things possible," he would now complete the circle by establishing himself (at least to the same degree) as a political reformer.

CHAPTER EIGHT

DOWN THE CHUTE

"A little picture of nightwork remaining among the excellent tables of their works."

—Bacon to Andrewes

While Bacon's new disciples throughout Europe were celebrating his efforts at the conquest of nature, his enemies at court were organizing to block his political reforms and planning ways and means of getting rid of him altogether. This was no easy task. He had risen to his present position according to the rules of the game which were not pretty perhaps, but which he had tried to lift at every opportunity. His hand had slipped only once, or maybe twice. Yet in the eyes of the world a reformer, or rather a reformer of Bacon's pretensions, is not permitted to make any slips at all. This would seem to be a harsh rule. However, it must be recalled that in this business the burden of proof is always on the reformer. If his air castles are built on a mud foundation, he cannot expect his contemporaries to take them seriously.

Bacon's chief fault was an old one, dating back to his first days as Lord Keeper. At that time, his office had been flooded with £7,000 worth of gifts, from "rich cabinets" to gold buttons, some of them from persons having cases pending before his court of Chancery. The rule was that a judge might receive gifts from such suitors so long as they were "for favors past and not for favors to come" and so long as they would not obligate the judge in his decrees. Bacon apparently had issued strict orders to his gentlemen assistants to accept only legal gifts.

But, by one device or another, they had managed to persuade him to accept several gifts that were clearly illegal. In some cases, they made him think that the gifts were for favors past, when, in fact, they were for favors to come. In other cases, they accepted gifts behind his back, entering into illegal bargains with suitors of which Bacon "was never made privy." Once when Bacon ruled against such a suitor, one of his gentlemen falsified the record. As Bacon later put it, "there was some shuffling between Mr. Shute [the gentleman] and the register in entering some order which I did distaste." Occupied as he was then with other matters, it was not until six months after this that he realized to what extent his gallants were taking advantage of him at which time he "cashiered" 16 of them "at a clip."

These facts had been related by Cromwell, one of Bacon's "cashiered gallants," to Sir Lionel Cranfield, the new leader of the anti-Bacon faction. And Cranfield had known just what to do with them.

Cranfield was one of the cleverest opponents Bacon had ever come up against. Commissioner of the Navy, Master of the Court of Wards, Bacon's successor as a leader in the House of Commons (Bacon was now presiding officer of the House of Lords), he had not merely risen by unscrupulous methods, but had boasted of them. "Tush man," he used to say to his critics, "I was bred in the city," which meant the same thing then that it does now. Starting as a London apprentice, he had become a successful merchant— after marrying one of Buckingham's relatives, a successful courtier and a successful administrator.

Differing so much in background and temperament from Bacon, it is not surprising that they should have taken an intense dislike for the other. No doubt Ben Jonson's remark had reached him "that My Lord Chancellor wringeth his speeches from the strings of his band, and the other councillors from the picking of their teeth." Also like Coke, who had referred to Bacon's college as a "ship of fools," he felt that the man's reputation as an innovator was largely undeserved. Had not he, Cranfield, just recently pared the King's household expenditures by £100,000 and his administrative expenses by £48,000? What had Bacon ever done to compare with this? In terms of immediate results, the answer was "nothing."

On the other hand, if Cranfield did not take Bacon's pretensions seriously, he was shrewd enough to realize that many other people did and that, under these circumstances, Cromwell's charges were almost wholly inadequate. After all, there was no evidence that Bacon, as Lord Chancellor, had ever been influenced by these illegal gifts; hence, the charges reflected more on Bacon's men than on Bacon personally. But suppose Cranfield could link the Lord Chancellor with some of the King's most unpopular measures, such as his monopoly system? Under this system, full powers over trade and industry were vested in the hands of a few favored courtiers who had badly abused their responsibilities. If he could establish Bacon's responsibility for these abuses, all the indignation that had lately been vented against the King and Buckingham on this count would now be vented against Bacon. The man's grandiose pretensions would be destroyed, and in the new atmosphere his neglect in the Court of Chancery would be severely punished.

Superficially, it would seem that Buckingham was more deeply implicated in the monopoly system than Bacon. Yet, here again, Cranfield did not altogether miss the mark. Buckingham's interest was more personal and direct, for several of his relatives actually depended on the monopolies for their livelihood. One of his cousins, Sir Giles Mompesson, charged with the administration of ale-houses, had found it profitable to convert them into bawdy houses. Two of his brothers were drawing £1,000 apiece yearly from the unpopular gold and silver thread monopoly.

On the other hand, Bacon's interest in monopolies was largely idealistic, believing them capable of stimulating his disciples to make new inventions and to provide them with protected markets, if and when these inventions were forthcoming. However, Bacon was one of the sponsors of the above-mentioned gold and silver thread monopoly. And after he had seen it abused, he had failed to get it repealed. "Monopolies are the cankers of all trading," he had told Buckingham on the eve of the new Parliament. "It would be better to take the credit for repealing them than the note for maintaining them." But for all his wise words he could not undo what he had already done.

Yet, when the monopoly issue was aired during those first weeks of the new Parliament (the opening day was February 5, 1621), it looked as though the Cranfield plan had miscarried, and that Buckingham, not Bacon, would be the victim. Coke was the leader of this anti-monopoly movement. Though restored to the Privy Council, he had been given no voice in the government. So now, as a member of the House of Commons, he followed up every scent of corruption fearlessly to its logical conclusion, with the rest of the members close behind him. Converting the House into a kind of Star Chamber, he sat in judgment on all Buckingham's friends and relatives who were implicated in the system. Within three weeks, he had sent one of them to the Tower and another into hiding. Soon perhaps it would be Buckingham's turn.

Cranfield may have felt that Coke's conduct of the case was misguided. But if so, he used it to his advantage by driving a wedge between the favorite and Bacon, his real target. By this time Buckingham had lost all of his suavity and self-assurance. When Cranfield (or one of his henchmen) called at Whitehall, Buckingham told him that if the prosecution continued, he would have the King dissolve Parliament. Cranfield assured him that Coke had done nothing that was not best for the King's honor, and that if he, Buckingham, would now disassociate himself from the monopolists, including his own brothers, and perhaps switch the blame to Bacon, he would be safe. Buckingham obviously had no relish for this scheme, for he had found Bacon to be an ornamental, harmless supporter. However, if he had to choose between saving his skin or Bacon's, clearly he had no choice at all.

Unwittingly, Bacon seconded Cranfield's advice. He, too, urged the favorite to dissociate himself from monopolists. But in this, he was only repeating the advice he had given him prior to the Parliament. As to his own share in the monopoly scandals, he was confident that his errors would be offset by his honest intentions. "I woo nobody," he said. "I do but listen. And I have doubt only of Sir Edward Coke, who I wish had some round caveat from the King" so that he, Bacon, could get started on his own reforms.

Three weeks before, when Sir Edward Sackville had asked whether a committee of the Commons could investigate his Court of Chancery, he had replied "that any man might speak freely anything concerning my court." In this case, his self-confidence was reinforced by the magnificent reception he had just received from both Houses of Parliament in honor of his *New Machine*. Had not the Lords acclaimed his genius to be "the straight line of nobleness without crooks or angles?" Had not the Commons reasserted their faith in him again, saying "I was the same man still, only honesty was turned into honor."

Nonetheless, on March 10, when it became known that Coke was planning to make specific charges against both Bacon and Buckingham, Bacon joined Buckingham in a premature self-defense before the Lords. The Lords declared them both out of order. Bacon apologized and withdrew from the chamber. But Buckingham could only be stopped at swordspoint, and even then, was so eager to be heard that he rushed from the Lords to the Commons where he had the order of business suspended on his behalf. His speech was vehement, but effective; so far as Bacon was concerned, it might very well have been dictated by Cranfield.

"I have always believed that monopolies were for the good of the country," he said. And if they had not turned out well, it was not his fault. First, he blamed his brothers. "If my father has begotten two sons to be grievances to the Commonwealth," he shouted, "I must tell them that the same father has begotten a third son who would help in punishing them." Then, he blamed the officials who had conceived the monopolies and authorized them, here hinting at Bacon.

Thus the stage was set for the second phase of the attack: the destruction of the Lord Chancellor himself. Little more was heard about the monopolies. But on March 14, the attention of the House was directed to Bacon's Court of Chancery, not only by Cranfield himself, but also by the Committee on Grievances that had been investigating it for the past month. As Cranfield well knew, the evidence was not very damaging. As yet, the committee had found only two cases in which gifts had been accepted illegally—two cases out of a total of more than seven thousand. Moreover, two of Bacon's men, Sir George Hastings and Sir Richard Young, had testified that it was they who had received the fees, not Bacon, and that Bacon either did not know about them, or had not been fully informed as to the circumstances. However, thanks to the debate over the monopolies, the self-built myth of Bacon's godhood had been effectively destroyed, and with the new charges added to the others, he was now transformed from a mythical god to a mythical monster.

Corruption in the Chancery—that is the "grievance of grievances" cried Coke, ponderously.

"The old rat has been hoarding his cheese" cried another member. The King should have created him Viscount St Nabal instead of Viscount St Albans, said still another, Nabal being a miser of Biblical fame.

One man characterized him as a minotaur, half-man, half-bull, "gormandizing and devouring all that came before him." Bacon's friends were now so much in the minority that they could hardly make themselves heard. One of them, with mistaken zeal, said that the Lord Chancellor was so noble a person that none but the King should be allowed to meddle with him.

To this, a spokesman of the opposite faction replied: "If he be gold [as you say], why should we fear to try him?"

Bacon was so stunned by this attack that he could not go on as the Lords' officer. But it was the sudden deflation of his reputation that upset him rather than any feeling of guilt. As a matter of fact, contemptuous as he was about administrative details, he seemed to have completely forgotten about the illegal gifts. "I know I have clean hands and a clean heart, and I hope a clean house for friends and servants," he wrote Buckingham. "But Job himself, or whosoever was the justest judge, by such hunting for matters against him as hath been used against me, may for a time seem foul, especially in a time when greatness is the mark and accusation the game." Even when he recalled the episode of his corruption, he still couldn't understand why it should be the occasion for so much abuse. "I see the way is already chalked out," he told Meautys, one of his servants. Though obviously Cranfield had planned the attack with demagogic skill, Bacon would defend himself with the truth on the mistaken belief that the truth was on his side.

On March 19, the charges against Bacon were sent to the House of Lords for a formal trial. At the same time, Buckingham presented them with a letter, setting forth Bacon's defense plan. Though inconvenienced by a "sickness of heart and back," Bacon was determined to devote all the strength at his command "to preserve my honor and fame as far as I am worthy." This, he assured them, would be an honest defense. "By the grace of God I shall not trick up an innocency with cavillations, but plainly and ingenuously (as your Lordships know my manner is) declare what I know and remember." Nor would he stand on any privilege of rank "for subterfuge or guiltiness."

He had but three requests. "First, that you will maintain me in your good opinion without prejudice until my cause be heard; secondly, that in regard I have sequestered my mind in great part from worldly matter, thinking of my answer in a higher court, your Lordships would give me some convenient time, according to the course of other courts, to advise with my counsel," and thirdly, that he be given the usual privilege of taking exception to hostile witnesses, producing his own witnesses and answering all complaints, severally and respectfully.

This letter was read twice, first by the clerk of the House, and then by the Lord Justice, who served as presiding officer in Bacon's absence. The reply was written by the Earl of Southampton. The Lords, he wrote, would sift the evidence until the Easter vacation, a week hence. Upon their return they would bring him to trial, at which time they would "be glad if his Lordship shall clear his honor therein." He assured Bacon that the trial would be conducted "according to the right rule of justice."

Meanwhile, Bacon's model research college had been rocked to its foundations. Not only had "his most judicious friends already given him for gone," not only had Buckingham proved himself a very uncertain protector, but now, one by one, his servants slipped away, as he put it, "like the flying of vermin when the house was falling." Some years later, Thomas Bushell, Bacon's technical assistant, would add his confession to those already given by Hastings and Young.

"Myself and others of his servants," Bushell wrote, "were the occasion of exhaling his virtue into a dark eclipse which God knows would have long endured had not we laid on his guiltless shoulders our base and execrable deeds." However, at this time the faint-hearted Bushell was in no mood for confession. Bushell's role in the ceremonies of the court was to precede the Lord Chancellor, carrying the mace. He had designed a special livery for himself "all covered with gold lace and full of gold buttons." It was now revealed that gold buttons were among the illegal gifts in the Chancery. So when the wits took up the cry "that his Lord's breeches made buttons and Bushell wore them," Bushell took to cover. Assuming the robes of a religious penitent, he buried himself in a solitary cell on the Isle of Wight.

Bacon, still clinging to his campaign of truth, refused to give up. When one of his servants told him sententiously, "It's time for me to look about," he replied, "I do not look about me, I look above me." Moreover, when his trial should come, he was prepared to stand up to his opponents like a Raleigh, or an Essex, or any other true Elizabethan. On similar occasions in the past, he already proved his capacity "to check the sallies of the soul on the steepest precipice and make it, like a well-trained horse, stop and turn." His only fear was that his body weakened "by continual attendance and business" and by the neglect of his "spring diet and physic" would once more "cast me down," which would be thought feigning or fainting. Returning to Gorhambury, his first act, apparently, was to draw up his will and testament, a precaution against a stroke; his second act was to make his peace with God. Meanwhile he had infected his remaining servants with his own optimism, and his friends were frankly amazed at this turnabout. Prince Charles was hunting at Berkhamsted, his country estate nearby. One day he "espied a coach attended with a goodly troop of horsemen, who were gathered to wait upon the Chancellor to his house at Gorhambury. At which the Prince smiled: 'Well, do what we can, this man scorns to go out like a snuff.' Commending his undaunted spirit and excellent parts; not without some regret that such a man should be falling off."

Bacon was so successful in bolstering his spirits that he may well have deceived himself into a false view of his prospects. For when he returned to London and settled down with his lawyer to look at the evidence against him, he realized how weak his case really was. Perhaps, he might have brazened it out, as Buckingham had done, and as other victims of the Parliamentary reign of terror were doing. Perhaps if he had done this he would have come out better in the long run. (It is interesting to note that another high official, Dr. Field, the Bishop of Llandaff, had also been implicated in the Bacon case. He had been charged with attempting to bribe one of Bacon's servants, which was a much more serious offense than Bacon's own. He was let off with an "admonition" from his ecclesiastical superiors.)

At any rate, Bacon now made a radical switch in his defense plans. On the one hand, he would not compromise with the truth. He had told the Lords that he would tell them "plainly and ingenuously what I know and remember." He now told the King to the same effect, that "I had rather be convicted as a briber than accused as a defender of bribes." On the other hand, he would not stand silently by while Cranfield used this one incident to distort the whole meaning of his career.

One sympathetic observer remarked at this time that "future ages will wonder how my Lord St. Albans (Bacon) could have fallen and how my Lord of Middlesex (Cranfield) could have risen." Bacon also wondered about it. Thus, in drawing up his "Humble Submission and Supplication" he appealed to the Lords as a kind of higher court to set his misdeeds against "the fair tables of his other works," and to judge him accordingly.

But what works? That was the question. The launching of his research college? "Had we performed and completely accomplished the whole of this enterprise, had we invented all things possible," we would not now have "to extol our own desserts," he had written in the *New Organon*. As it was, he had done nothing but "call in others to assist us in our labors." And it would be very difficult to explain once again how enormously the human race would profit and how much improvement there would be in "men's bread and wine" as a result of his pioneering work. As to his political reforms, here he faced the same difficulty. Throughout his whole career, he had worked directly or indirectly to establish a model government appropriate to the new era of "man's empire over nature."

"I have been no avaricious oppressor of the people," he told the King. "I have been no haughty or intolerable or hateful man in my conversation or carriage. I have never been author of any immoderate counsel." But apart from a few meaningless statutes or ordinances, such as his anti-duelling ordinance, his reforms existed only as blueprints in his desk. Here again, he would be "extoling our own desserts" to a skeptical audience.

However, as yet, Bacon was unwilling to face the realities of his situation, and in this crisis, a strange and impossible solution occurred to him. If the Lords would put an end to this reign of terror, and if they would let him carry on with his own program of reforms, he would prove to them just how public-spirited he was. Naturally, he did not expect them to continue him as Lord Chancellor. His "humble desire," he said, was that the King would accept his resignation. This would serve not only for an "expiation of my faults, but also for an example for [the next] 400 years."[15] Thereafter, the greatness of a judge shall be "no sanctuary or protection of guiltiness" and "judges will fly from anything that is in the likeness of corruption as from a serpent." But at least they might let him carry on in some lesser capacity— as a Privy Councillor or as a member of the Lords. In that case, he said, "I hope I shall be a new man and shall reform things out of feeling more than another can do out of my example."

---

15   2021 marked four hundred years since the time of Bacon's statement.

This, Bacon admitted, was an extraordinary request. To adopt it, they would have to exercise more discretion than other courts usually did. However, there were two considerations that might weigh with them. In the first place, he wrote, "you all sit upon one high stage, and therefore you cannot but be more sensible of the changes of the world, and of the fall of any from high place." By the same token, you must know "that the questioning of men in eminent place hath the same terror, though not the same rigor, with the punishment." This fact, he went on, was recognized in the military code of the Romans. Through bitter experience, the Romans had learned that it was not necessary to destroy one erring general simply to keep the others in line. By a system of admonitions they could maintain discipline without the loss of their best men. Neither will your Lordships forget that there are "crimes of the time" as well as "crimes of the man."

Clearly, it was only through some strong action on the part of the King that this impossible plan could be accepted. The King knew more about Bacon's good intentions than anybody because, according to Bacon, he had done more than anybody else to frustrate them. The King later wrote: "Howsoever (Bacon) offended in judicature, yet in matter of counsel we found him faithful and very careful and diligent, running courses entire and direct for the good of the service." Moreover, he had lately become so fond of his Lord Chancellor that at the onset of Cranfield's attack, he had broken down and wept. (Later he would scold both Cranfield and Buckingham on this account).

"You are fools," the King said. "You are making a rod with which you yourselves will be scourged." But now, although he did urge Prince Charles and the favorite to defend Bacon's honor, he personally maintained a posture of strict neutrality. These two "great persons" could not save Bacon. Perhaps, indeed, they hurt him. At any rate, when the great majority of the Lords rejected his so-called confession, because as one said he was trying to be "the judge in his own case—to prescribe his own punishment and his own sentence," they withdrew their support and joined with the others in demanding a "full and particular confession."

So long as there was any hope at all of vindicating himself by actual works of invention or reform, Bacon's spirits had been high. But now that this hope had gone, now that his pretensions were deflated beyond repair, and he saw himself exposed before his contemporaries, if not later ages, as a corruptionist of the worst stripe, he suffered an almost complete collapse. His perennial headache became so bad that, according to his own diagnosis "it must grow to a congelation and so to lethargy or to break and so to mortal fever and death." Moreover, if death had come to him at this time, he said, it would not have been "unwelcome."

The Lords had given him five days to send them "such confession and submission as he intended to make." He waited until the last day, then somehow steeled himself to read the articles of the charge, now numbering 28. Of these he found that 11 concerned gifts that were clearly legal, 3 concerned loans that may or may not have been improper, 3 involved gifts that were matters of public record, and 3 referred to incidents that had completely escaped his memory. Seven other articles indicated that he had in fact accepted improper gifts. But the nature of his offense was best summed up in his reply to the final article. "It was a great fault in me that I looked no better to my servants," he confessed.

Thereafter, Bacon followed the formalities of his conviction with utter detachment. Immediately after his final confession had been read to the Lords, a committee of 12 Lords called on him at York House. "They conceived it to be an ingenuous and full confession," they said, and they asked "whether the signature were his, if so, whether he would stand to it or no."

"My Lords," he replied from behind the curtains of his bedstead, "it is my act, my hand, my heart. I beseech your Lordships, be merciful to a broken reed." The next day another delegation of Lords called on him, this time a committee of four of his closest supporters—Arundel, Pembroke, the Lord Stewart, and the Lord Treasurer, appointed by the King, to take back the Great Seal, the emblem of his office. They expressed their regret for this painful duty, saying they "wished it had been better with him."

"The worse the better," he said. "By the King's great favor I received the Great Seal; by my own great fault I have lost it." Soon after they had left, he was advised by the Gentleman Usher and the Sergeant at Arms that the Lords were prepared to give sentence, that all the judges would be there in their robes, that the Lower House had been sent for, and that if Bacon attended, all due respect would be shown him save that since he no longer had the seal, his entrance would not be heralded by the mace. But Bacon could not be rallied.

By an almost unanimous vote, the Lords agreed: 1) that he should be fined £40,000, 2) imprisoned in the Tower, during the King's pleasure, 3) prohibited from holding any office, place or employment in the state, and 4) forbidden to sit in Parliament again or come within 10 miles of the court. In the light of his actual offense, this sentence seems to have been unnecessarily hard. However, so great was their feeling against this fallen idol that he was lucky they didn't make it any worse—that they didn't strip him of his titles of nobility, for example. This additional punishment had actually been proposed by the Earl of Southampton. Bacon was "unfit to be a constable," much less to be a nobleman, he declared.

However, now at last, Bacon's friends managed to bring this idol smashing within reasonable limits. After all, said Spencer, "a man may be attainted for corruption and yet, his honor remain."

"So clear and ingenuous a confession would have been impossible for any man of the baser sort," added the Earl of Cambridge. When "the lords spiritual," said that they, too, believed in his integrity, Bacon was restored again to his rightful stature as neither a god nor a beast, but an extraordinarily imaginative and fallible human being.

Bacon's few days in the Tower at the end of May marked the high point of his agony. "Death, I thank God, is far from being unwelcome to me," he had told Buckingham. "But to die before the time of his Majesty's grace, and in this disgraceful place, is even the worst that could be." This message Buckingham passed on to the King, who promptly had him released. Also prior to his return to Gorhambury, he was permitted to rest up in Sir John Vaughan's house in suburban Fulham. At this point, one would have thought that Bacon would renounce his great pretensions once and for all, and remain quietly in the shadows. But the man was truly indestructible.

No longer able to establish "man's empire over nature" by actual works in his own time, he would help his disciples do it by works of the imagination. This adjustment was not achieved without many regrets and occasional backslidings. But every day, it seemed, he felt better. His headache disappeared as rapidly as it had come. His shooting pains left him. The courage that had failed him at his trial now came welling up inside him. On June 7, a week after his release from the Tower, he informed Prince Charles that "the sweet air and loving usage of this house hath already much revived my languishing spirits."

Meanwhile, to set the record straight on the political front, he wrote a full-length portrait of the model king that he had been holding up before James all these years. Oddly enough, this model was no imaginary figure created out of his head, but one of James' own forebears, King Henry VII, who had died more than a century before—a rather crotchety character compared with his son, Henry VIII, but as Bacon said, an extraordinarily wise one for those times. Bacon had already accumulated some notes on this model king, and these were now enriched after a study of Sir Robert Cotton's original manuscripts.

The portrait itself, which was begun immediately after his return to Gorhambury, was completed in about four months. A book of 350 pages, it was hailed at once as a masterpiece, and has since been recognized as a landmark in the evolution of scientific biography. Bacon had no illusions, of course, that James would be so inspired by his work that he would turn over a new leaf. But certainly "it was not amiss" for Prince Charles to have a look at one of these "ancient pieces." And if Prince Charles learned nothing from it, then other kings in future ages might find it stimulating and instructive.

Prince Charles learned nothing from this work. 28 years later, by ignoring Bacon's model, the Prince, then King Charles I, would lose his throne and his life. However, in writing it, Bacon undoubtedly felt better. For the first time, he realized how grossly he had deceived himself, believing that he could reform this court. For the first time, he realized what a favor Cranfield had done him in relieving him from an impossible predicament. Had he invented some drug for "increasing and exalting" men's "intellectual faculties" (and some such invention as this was on his scientific agenda) perhaps, then, his reforms might have been practical. But without the drug he had simply been dreaming his life away. Henceforth, he would never quibble about his conviction. "I was the justest judge that was in 30 years," he would say, "and yet it was the justest sentence that was in 300." And when he came to answer for himself before God he composed a remarkable prayer to the same effect: "Thousand have been my sins and ten thousand my transgressions ... But (worst of all) I confess before thee that I am a debtor to thee for the gracious talent of thy gifts and graces. This I have neither put into a napkin, nor put it, as I ought, to exchangers, where it might have made best profit, but misspent it in things for which I was least fit."

Chapter Nine

ESCAPE TO THE FUTURE

"It is true greatness to have in one the frailty of a man and
the security of a god."

—*Seneca*

Throughout his whole career, the prospect of a research college producing "works of power and utility" had been as essential to Bacon as a
wand to a wizard or a cauldron to a witch. Yet if he could not organize such
a college when he had the enormous prestige of the Chancery behind him,
how much less were his chances of organizing it now that he was broken and
in disgrace? The King, perhaps, was still friendly. But, so far as any contributions were concerned, his hands were tied by the harsh terms of Bacon's
sentence. Bacon's converts were so demoralized, that with few exceptions,
they no longer corresponded with him. Ben Jonson, one of the exceptions,
wrote: "In his adversity I ever prayed that God would give him strength, for
greatness he could not want."

As to his model college at Gorhambury, it was running down at the
heels. Weeds were growing in the botanical gardens; the pondyards were reverting to the "desert" from which he had originally converted them. Since
the fountains no longer worked, the ponds themselves were covered with
"green and red discoloration," with "mossiness and putrefaction." Under
pressure from creditors, bit by bit, both Verulam House and Gorhambury

House were being stripped of their "feathers." Worst of all, in the general rout of his servants, his establishment had been reduced from a hundred men to maybe a dozen or less. Most loyal of these were Dr. Rawley, his chaplain and secretary, and Peter Böener, a Dutch apothecary. However, being unable to support them, he tried (unsuccessfully) to get Rawley placed as chaplain to Dr. Williams, his successor as Lord Keeper; and two years later he permitted Böener to return to Holland.

Yet the situation was, by no means, hopeless. Through the publications of the *New Machine*, he had scattered his seed across the face of Europe; sooner or later, this seed "would bud anew." Just when this rebirth would take place he could not say. At times now, he was willing to face up to the possibility that his disciples "would take an age, perhaps a whole age, to prove [his enterprise], and numerous ages to execute [it]." But there was also the possibility that he could stimulate them both to prove it and partially execute it within his own lifetime. If not, he would carry on his pioneering work single-handed. If need be, he told Dr. Rawley, he would be not only an architect of this building, "but a workman and a laborer, digging the clay and burning the brick, and more than that, gathering the straw and stubble over all the fields to burn the brick withal."

Meanwhile, Bacon sent the King full reports on his financial situation. It was extraordinarily tangled. During his four years as Lord Chancellor, he had received about £10,000 a year in salary and fees and an additional £10,000 in investments and rents. A total of at least £50,000, this was an enormous sum. In Queen Elizabeth's time, it would have supported an army of 6,000 foot and 1,000 horse in the field for six months. But all of this and more, Bacon had spent on his college directly or indirectly. Now he owed £24,000 for private debts incurred in the same period, as well as the £40,000 fine that had been slapped on him as part of his sentence.

In September 1621, following his trial, King James had made certain legal arrangements to relieve him from his creditors, if not from his debts. But his situation was still intolerable. In July he said he was living "upon the scraps of my former fortunes and I shall not be able to hold out longer." In September, he told the King flatly that he simply could not go on without help from the Crown. "The honors which your Majesty hath done me have put me above the means to get my living and the misery I am fallen into hath put me below the means to subsist as I am. . . . Let your suppliant that aspireth but to live to study be not put to study to live."

Bacon was not asking for charity. His enterprise being for the "betterment of men's bread and wine" deserved public support. And if the King was not yet ready to accept this, then he might regard the subsidy as payment for some of Bacon's more conventional works, such as his *King Henry VII*. On the latter basis, apparently, the old King approved the subsidy.

Unfortunately, Bacon's fall had been followed by his arch-enemy's rise. Cranfield was now Lord Treasurer, and second only to Buckingham in the King's favor. From this perch he did everything he could, not merely to prevent Bacon's relief, but also to put him out of business. When the King decided in Bacon's favor, Cranfield urged James "to meddle with no pardon for the Viscount St. Albans" on the grounds that this would alienate Parliament. When this didn't work, Cranfield spread the rumor that Bacon had made £1,000,000 in illegal fees in the Chancery, and that therefore, he had no need for any subsidy. At the same time, he had all of Bacon's other sources of income stopped.

Since Bacon's financial condition was exactly as he had said it was, this was an almost mortal blow. Increasingly now, Bacon was forced to strip his palaces of "jewels and plate and the like" to defray operating expenses. And when Cranfield had squeezed him to the point where he had "scarce bread for himself and his family," he offered to buy one or the other of these palaces on terms very favorable to himself. In September 1622, in a formal petition over Cranfield's head, Bacon informed the King of these chicanaries. But before the King could do anything about them, Bacon had already lost York House and abandoned Gorhambury House, expecting to lose this too, at any time.

One can well imagine how terrible a blow it was for Bacon to leave Gorhambury. Not long before, according to Aubrey, his neighbors, hearing how much he was in debt, had come to him "with a motion to buy Oakwood from him," Oakwood being a wood adjoining the main part of his estate. He had refused outright saying, "I will not part with my feathers."

About this time the Provost of Eton College became ill, and Bacon could think of no better place to switch to transfer his activities. Eton was then, as it is now, the most fashionable of England's grammar schools. In his mind's eye he could see this school made over into a research college, better even than Gorhambury. The gardens would be devoted to experimental purposes, the "wits and pens" of its faculty should be dedicated to his Natural History project, and the young earls and viscounts would be trained henceforth to "bestow their wealth and magnificence" upon such works. In his appeal to the King, Bacon did not mention this aspect of the case—perhaps he didn't have to.

At any rate, the King saw at once that Eton would make a "pretty cell" for Bacon's fortune. Also he agreed that the appointment was politically feasible, since the job had previously been held by non-entities and involved no cost to the Crown. Yet here again, the King's promise meant nothing. The King had turned over all such appointments to Buckingham, and Buckingham by this time had also become strongly infected with the Cranfield poison. After keeping his old adviser waiting and hoping for seven months, Buckingham finally informed him that the job had been promised elsewhere and that this promise could not be broken save for a few well beyond Bacon's means. As it turned out, the job went not to that man, but still another, Sir Henry Wotton, one of Bacon's most ardent admirers. But whether or not this gave Bacon any comfort, we don't know.

"For quiet and the better to hold out," he now moved the rump of his model college to his old rooms at Gray's Inn. The next step in his program was the great Natural History project. In its original conception this was to have been a scientific inventory including not only "all normal phenomena of heavenly bodies, meteors, earth and sea," but much more of "nature artificially delimited by hand." Here at Gray's Inn, without any facilities for collecting and examining specimens, indeed with hardly any facilities at all except a garden that he had planted there, he obviously couldn't get very far with it.

However, the classical works on the subject, the Natural Histories of Aristotle and Pliny, were close at hand in his library. These and other less ancient works, might serve as his source materials. By the exercise of his natural insight sharpened by his "continual conversation with nature," he might bring them up-to-date, rejecting all unscientific facts and explaining all unexplained wonders in more plausible terms. Pliny's work, it should be noted, was a natural for Bacon, being full of fantastic reports about "dragons ten fathoms long," noble lions that eat men rather than women, and beasts that eat corn at night in the fields, wild dogs with human hands and feet, etc. However, it must be added that many of Bacon's corrections are equally farfetched to the modern eye. The negroes' dark skin, for example, he explained as a mere matter of sunburn.[16]

Bacon was well aware of the inadequacy of this project. He called it "an indigested heap of particulars" without "that lustre that books cast into methods have." However, like his inconclusive experiments on heat, it might serve as a model and stimulant for his disciples. Once his *Natural History* was published, no doubt there would be another great acclamation as with the publication of the *New Machine*. "The design would bud anew." And the little college at Gray's Inn would be augmented with hundreds of eager new converts.

Every evening, according to his apothecary, he worked over the texts, reading and making notes until midnight when everyone else had retired except his valet. Early the next morning he rose, and gathering his assistants around him, dictated to them "what he had invented and composed during the night." In the afternoons, while his other servants were checking the accuracy of his quotations, he walked back and forth in the Gray's Inn gardens. Dr. Rawley followed close at his heels with ink horn and pen. Whenever some "present notion" darted into his mind, Rawley would set it down.

As time went on, Bacon's difficulties mounted. Friends who once had been proud to supply him with beer that was "liking his pallet" now ordered their butlers to turn him away from the door. Soon his wife Alice would run off with Sir John Underhill, her gentleman usher. The couple were married after Bacon's death and, according to Aubrey, she made Sir John "deaf and dumb with too much Venus." During his hey-day, Bacon had "prosecuted" her with coaches and coach geldings, with gifts of armor, rich chairs and marble tables. Also of course, he had made her a Viscountess. But now that they lived in "the base court of adversity where almost nobody will be seen stirring," there was nothing left apparently to hold her to her "lord." Yet so absorbed was Bacon with his *Natural History* that except on such rare occasions as when he cut his wife out of his will, he hardly noticed what the

---

16   This book was written in the late 1950s when this word choice would have still been in use.

world was doing to him. Never before had he shown such complete mastery over his emotions. And "if miracles be the command of nature," or over nature in a man's self, as he said in his *Essays*, by this performance he had certainly achieved one of them.

How far, indeed, Bacon had risen above outside circumstances is shown by the following incident, which was told years later by Dr. Rawley to Bishop Tenison, one of Bacon's earliest anthologists. "One day," wrote Tenison, "his Lordship was dictating [to Dr. Rawley]" some of the experiments for his *Natural History*. The same day he had sent a friend to court to receive for him a final answer, touching the effect of a grant which had been made to him by King James. He had hitherto only hoped for it, and hope deferred; he was desirous to know the event of the matter, and to be freed one way or other from the suspense of his thoughts.

His friend, returning, told him plainly that he must thenceforth despair of that grant how much soever his fortunes needed it. "Be it so," said his Lordship, and then he dismissed his friend very cheerfully with thankful acknowledgement of his services. His friend being gone, he came straightway to Dr. Rawley, and said: "Well, sir, yon business won't go on. Let us go on with this, for this is in our power." And then he "dictated to him afresh for some hours without the lowest hesitation of speech or discernible interruption of thought."

Meanwhile, the affairs at court were going badly. The bounty that the King had withheld from Bacon was showered on Buckingham (now the Duke of Buckingham) at the rate of about £40,000 per annum. And Buckingham was putting on one of the dizziest shows of mismanagement England had ever seen. For six years the government had stood uncertainly and reluctantly as the leader of a Protestant coalition against Catholic Spain. In 1623, in a last ditch effort to avoid war, Buckingham escorted Prince Charles to Madrid, and there attempted to arrange his marriage to the Spanish Infanta Maria. The two Englishmen travelled incognito, disguised respectively as Mr. Smith and Mr. Brown. From start to finish the whole affair was ill-fated: Bacon described it as "more like a fable" of the poets "than a mature piece of diplomacy." But this was not all. When the negotiations broke down, Buckingham suddenly found himself at war not merely with one major enemy but with two, that is to say with Catholic France as well as with Catholic Spain. And it was then he discovered apparently for the first time that England was not prepared for any wars at all. Her Navy could no longer raid and devastate the Spanish coast as in the days of Elizabeth and Essex. Her Army was so poorly equipped that half the men of a continental expeditionary force froze to death before they made contact with the enemy.

For one misstep Bacon had been made the goat for all the tyrannies and errors of this bankrupt government. But now, it was plain that other councillors were much more at fault than he, and one by one, they, too, were tried before the High Court of Parliament. In February 1624, it was Cranfield's turn. Charges of corruption were brought against him; his friends at court abandoned him, and ironically his sentence read very much like Bacon's. Two years later, they passed on to Buckingham. The House of Commons impeached him on 13 counts. They couldn't convict him, but in discrediting him, they inadvertently set the stage for his murder shortly afterward at the hands of a disappointed office-seeker.

King James' own person was protected from such indignities by the majesty of his office. But he was terribly offended by the loss of his most trusted councillors and was terribly disillusioned by the collapse of his most cherished policies. He wept continuously now, and moved restlessly from one palace to another like a hunted animal. "Things came to me raw as if I had never heard of them before," he wrote near the end. "I was as disappointed of my ends as if I had been waked out of a dream." On March 27, 1625, he died of kidney failure. The Prince of Wales succeeded him as Charles I.

The logic of these events, Bacon thought, dictated his recall to the Privy Council, or at least, a full pardon for his offense. Yet the events themselves were vindication enough. With the hollowness of the James regime now so clearly demonstrated, posterity could see what Bacon had been up against in trying to commit them to the conquest of nature. Also, posterity could do what Parliament had failed to do—namely, to set his failings in the proper perspective. To make doubly sure about this, Bacon ordered his men to help him collect and preserve all the pertinent records of his life. Nothing of any consequences was left out; he had nothing to hide. The whole fantastic epic of his triumphs and of his failures constituted a "fatality" which he would not have changed if he had his life to live over again.

His major works, including *The Advancement of Learning* and the ever popular *Essays*, were expanded and translated from English into Latin. This was done on the mistaken theory that English was changing so fast as to "play the bankrupt with books." His letters and speeches were neatly pack-aged and deposited in "cabinets, boxes or presses." The speeches were of obvious importance. But the letters, he said, were even more important, "for they contain more of natural sense than speeches, more ripeness than es-says," and when arranged in the proper order would explain his connection with his times. Even his witticisms were preserved.

In the fall of 1624, he had Dr. Rawley take down three hundred of them, which he rattled off from memory—some of them of his own com-position, others that he remembered from his reading, and still others from such great contemporaries as Raleigh, Coke, and Queen Elizabeth. When he was finished, Bacon was embarrassed by his own candor. "My father used to say that a man is a fool that will lose his friend for his wit," he told Rawley. "But he is an even greater fool that will lose his friend for another's wit." However, he let the remarks stand as he remembered them.

Meanwhile, despite these interruptions, the Natural History project was taking shape at the rate roughly of a volume a year. His schedule called for a book a month on such subjects as winds, density, and rarity, heaviness and lightness, sulphur, mercury and salt, life and death, etc. Even at the lesser rate this was a tremendous undertaking, running to more than a thousand printed pages. In the long run, this apparently futile work would find its mark. More than two hundred years later, when Charles Darwin boarded the *Beagle* and set out on the voyage that led to the doctrine of evolution, he did not hesitate to credit Bacon's *Natural History* as part of his inspiration. Yet, unfortunately at this time it fell dead, and Bacon could not conceal his disappointment.

"Men are so set to despise the means of their own good," he said, that if he didn't carry on, nobody else would. There was no blaze of scientific enthusiasm, no great influx of converts and correspondents, no appreciable interest anywhere in the revival of his college. On the contrary, it looked now as though his converts were on the wane rather than on the rise. In the great Universities, the anti-scientific professors were once more in the saddle. In 1628, one would be forced to resign "for speaking too much in defense of liberty," and the lectureship founded in Bacon's name would be abandoned.

Sometime in 1623 or 1624, Bacon dreamed of the finale that he might have had if King James had been more cooperative, or if his converts had rallied to him in sufficient numbers. To put it mildly, this was an amazing dream—a mixture of 20th or 21st century technology with lavish 17th century fol-de-rol. His Gorhambury facilities had miraculously grown from a few aviaries and botanical gardens into a complete scientific city fully staffed with laboratory workers and humming "with power from violent streams and cataracts."

Each department of science had its own special building and in each of these was some prophetic gadget. The "sound houses" boasted hearing aids "which set to the ear do further the hearing greatly," and telephones whereby "the voice is conveyed in trunks and pipes in strange lines and distances." The optical shops (or "perspective houses") were equipped with something that looked like electric lights, for he had "divers means of producing light originally from diverse bodies." His furnaces were so hot being "in imitation of the sun's and heavenly bodies' heat" that nothing but an atomic explosion could have accounted for them. His refrigerators were somewhat primitive by contrast with the other installations. He could think of no way to get low temperature save by digging a ½ mile deep under mountains 2½ miles high. He probably got better results from the observation towers that he erected as high above sea level as the caves were below it. They were manned by monks, chosen for their capacity for hardship and solitude. Undoubtedly his masterpiece was his weather factory. In it he could produce snow, hail, rain, thunder and lightning, and "some artificial rains" unknown even to us.

For the first time, now, the enormous importance of his enterprise was visible, not merely to a handful of wits, but to the entire nation. The King was amazed and delighted. As a matter of fact the whole position of Bacon and the court was now reversed. Instead of his appealing to the King for funds, the King came to him or sent emissaries. The people were even more enchanted. When he made a "progress" through the principal cities of the realm, they lined the streets to catch a glimpse of him.

Nor did he disappoint them. For, in keeping with his belief that inventors outranked politicians, he showed more feathers even than he had shown in his induction as Lord Keeper. He was dressed much as he had been then, with black robes over an undergarment of white linen, with velvet peach-colored shoes, though instead of his judicial hat, he wore something that looked like a "helmet or a Spanish montera." He rode in a magnificent chariot made of cedar and studded with sapphires and rubies. His two closest assistants cleared the way for him; Dr. Rawley carried a crozier of balm wood, Peter Böener a pastoral staff. Fifty of his other assistants followed immediately in his train while "the officer and principals of the companies of the city" took up the rear.

Had Bacon been as vindictive and grasping as he had been lately described, he might have pushed this dream one step further. He might have marched on London, routed his enemies, captured the King, and seized the reins of government in his own hands. There is no question that his midget submarines ("boats for going under water") would have made quick work of the "rotten hoys" that then constituted the Royal Navy. His flame-throwers with their "wild-fires burning in water and unquenchable" would have routed an army of muskets and pikes. Certainly, at the first sight of one of his planes built in "imitation of the flights of birds," the palace guard would have fled for cover.

Yet throughout his life, Bacon never had any serious designs on the court other than to get them to cooperate in founding a research college. Now that his college had come into its own (in his dream), his attitude towards the court was one of compassion and aloofness. Indeed, as the dream further unfolded, he looked more like the father of some benevolent religious order than like a would-be dictator.

Save for some of the more destructive weapons, which presumably he kept within the college to reinforce its dignity and freedom, everything that he had discovered was published and readily available for use both by the government and the general public. His "dispensatories," or shops of medicine, were operated like modern free clinics. Likewise his other medical facilities—the caves three miles deep that were used in the cure of certain diseases, and the "artificial wells and fountains" filled with a special "water of paradise" that was "very soverign for health and prolongation of life."

His factories not only provided instruments for his own use, but also the most up-to-date gadgets for the market. In its haberdasheries in Paul's Cross, elegant garments of gold and silver thread had been replaced with modern ones made of synthetic fabrics (like rayon and nylon). In the music shops were recordings of the human voice "reflected and tossed as it were" (perhaps, recordings of crooners), and also something we haven't sufficiently thought of—recordings of the "voices and notes of beasts and birds." The farmers were guaranteed fair weather by Bacon's weather making equipment.

However, every 12 years he went the rounds of the Kingdom with his assistants on a kind of technical mission. On this mission, he gave the farmers a "divination," covering the period until his next visit, of "diseases, swarms of harmful creatures, scarcity, tempests, earthquakes, great inundations, comets, and temperatures of the year." At the same time, he inspected and advised on all public health measures—particularly on all measures instituted for "the prevention and remedy" of plagues.

This dream was altogether so delightful from Bacon's point of view, it contrasted so sharply with his actual plight that during his few remaining years, he hardly ever woke from it. Even when he had set it down in the *New Atlantis*—incidentally, a book that was published posthumously in 1627, and that would probably do more to help the research movement than all his other books combined—even then, he couldn't shake it off. In the *New Atlantis*, Gorhambury was disguised as Salomon's House; England became Bensalem, a remote island in the Pacific: no king was ever described or even mentioned, and he referred to himself simply as the "Father." But there is no doubt that its installations and inventions were precisely the ones that he had been hoping for all his life. If only he could work one of these many scientific miracles! And if all rational hope of such a finale was gone there was still the off chance that he would stumble upon it by accident.

Suppose, for example, he could work the miracle of a prolonged life! The reason for his choice was obvious enough. In the first place, by living 50 or 100 years beyond the normal threescore and ten, he was sure of attracting a tremendous amount of attention both to himself and to his college. In the second place, if he could work this miracle, he wouldn't have to work any others. For time was on his side, and within a century, if not sooner, his converts perhaps would work the others for him. Following a prolonged illness in the winter of 1622–23, he pushed all other studies aside and gave it top priority. "The subject is so extremely profitable and important," he told his men, that "even the slightest loss of time [from it] should be accounted precious."

At first glance, it would seem that here once again, as in his youth, Bacon was taking a leaf out of the book of his hated rivals, the alchemists. The alchemists claimed that "with a morning's draft of potable gold" or "the flesh of serpents," or by covering a man from head to foot with an ointment, they could make him live to be three hundred "free from all diseases save swellings on the soles of his feet." However, in Bacon's case, though his ends were identical with the "quacks," his means were thoroughly scientific—and so far ahead of the times that we have only just begun to catch up with him.

In the first place, he said, for the "prolongation of life" a wholly new branch of medicine must be founded with its own objectives and its own techniques. Physicians must raise their sights above "sordid cures." They must distinguish between "what conduces to health and what to a long life." At a recent American medical convention, in much the same language, physicians were again urged to "change their practice from today's emergency medicine to one of preventive medicine." The next step in his analysis is probably a little too fanciful for modern taste. But it is suggestive all the same. Men die of old age, Bacon argued, because their repair facilities break down. Some of their vital parts are repaired successfully, some unsuccessfully, so that after a certain age, "the human body begins to suffer that torture of Mezebtius wherby the living dies in the embrace of the dead." However, by a "variety of remedies" and by "a proper continuation and intermixture thereof," this breakdown might conceivably be postponed for a century or more.[17]

What remedies should be used? Neither Bacon nor any of his disciples since then has ever quite put his finger on them. But Bacon had some very definite ideas on the subject. "Since embalming preserves dead bodies," he asked, "Why shouldn't something of like kind preserve live ones?" Bacon not only asked the question, but attempted to answer it, using himself as guinea pig. That is to say, he tried literally to embalm himself, or to put himself on ice, as we would say. He went about it systematically from one "vital part" to another.

To preserve his stomach, he adopted a diet so prepared that it may more easily "insinuate and require less digestion." This is what we would call a bland diet. "To restore the bloom of the body," once weekly at 7 p.m. he took a mild laxative. This might be either some strained fruit juice or a quarter ounce of rhubarb soaked in wine. In either case, he said it would guarantee results in four hours. "For the freshening of the blood," he took

---

17   Interesting to note that venture investments in technology to extend human life have been funded by current billionaires—with examples including Jeff Bezos, Larry Page, Larry Ellison, and Peter Thiel.

baths daily in moderately warm water filled with whey and roses. This was similar to the "water of paradise" that was to have been developed in his scientific college, "very sovereign for health and prolongation of life." If he could have dug one of those caves three miles below sea level, which were also "very sovereign for health and prolongation of life," no doubt he would have buried himself in it for a century or until his disciples came to dig him out.

Proper mental adjustment was also important to "the preservation of the spirit," and since he was wholly immersed in his scientific work this was just about right. He had a definite goal in life—one that was neither so high as to cause frustration or so low as to lose his interest. "My zeal and constancy of mind had not waxed old in this design, nor after so many years grown cold and indifferent," he told Father Fulgentio, one of his Italian disciples. Moreover, in this dark hour when his research college was reduced to its lowest estate, the world still could not deprive him of the means, imaginary or otherwise, of reaching that goal. As a matter of fact, he now reversed his former championship of the active over the contemplative life. It is business with its "anxieties and elations" that burns up a man's spirits, he said, while quiet contemplation of "the variety of nature unbounded, the stars, the heroic virtues and the like," helps to preserve them. For this reason, he said, philosophers generally lived longer than politicians and men of business.

Now for all we know, this regimen might have kept Bacon alive for many years. Unfortunately, he had been late in adopting it; after so many years in politics, his "spirits" were almost completely burned out.

In early April 1626, accompanied by Dr. Witherborne, King Charles' physician, he left Gray's Inn for his old home at Gorhambury. There had been a heavy snowfall. Bacon had stayed up late the night before speculating on the utility of snow for producing alloys ("new artificial metals"), prolonging life and preserving food. The subject had enormous possibilities. He mentioned them now to his companion. When their coach reached Highgate Hill, about halfway to Gorhambury, he asked the other whether a chicken stuffed inside with snow would be better preserved than one packed in salt. The Doctor gave a tentative answer.

"Tush man, will you tell any man's disease before you have examined him?" Bacon demanded. "So is it with nature." At the nearest cottager's house, Bacon stopped, bought a chicken, and had its gizzard and guts removed and packed with snow. Just how any results could have been expected from such a casual test is not clear. But shortly afterwards both men agreed that "the experiment succeeded excellently well."

Meanwhile Bacon complained that he was not feeling well. "Whether it were stone, or some surfeit [or cold], or indeed a touch of all three," neither he nor the Doctor could tell. But he "was taken with such a fit of casting [vomiting] that he could not return to Gray's Inn." Luckily, one of Bacon's friends, the Earl of Arundel, had a house not far off, and there they went. Arundel, himself, was nowhere about. For some ridiculous offense—because his son had made an imprudent marriage—he, too, had lost favor with the court and he, too, had been sent to the Tower. In his stead, the housekeeper made the two men welcome, assigning the best bed in the house to the former Lord Chancellor.

Bacon was so sick now that he couldn't "steadily hold a pen." But when materials were brought to him, he wrote a personal note of thanks to his absent host. "I was like to have had the fortune of [the Roman] Pliny [whose *Natural History*, Bacon was then re-editing]" "who lost his life by trying an experiment about the burning of the mountain Vesuvius . . . Your housekeeper is very diligent about me, which I assure myself your Lordship will not only pardon towards me, but think the better of him for it. And I kiss your noble hands for the welcome I am sure you give me to it."

Arundel's manor was filled with perhaps the finest collection of Greek and Roman statuary in England; many of its treasures had been sent from Italy by Bacon's former secretary, Sir Tobie Matthew. Just as Gorhambury with its orchards and bird sanctuaries was the prototype of our scientific botanical gardens, so Arundel House was the prototype of a modern art museum. On a previous visit to this house, in more prosperous times, Bacon had been so impressed by its many marble nudes that he had cried "Behold the Resurrection." In this delightful setting, Bacon settled down for a long convalescence. His secretaries and assistants were sent for, his books were brought to him, and at every opportunity his scientific work was continued. Unfortunately, as one of his disciples put it, death was a law of nature, and though Bacon had "conned all the mysteries of nature," he himself would have "to fulfill nature's decree." The bed the housekeeper had assigned him, the best in the house, had not been occupied for a long time. A warming pan did not remove the dampness. Within a week, according to Aubrey, he caught "a great cold whereby the defluxion of rheum fell so plentifully upon his breast" that he was suffocated. He died early in the morning of April 9, surrounded by a corporal's guard of his most faithful disciples.

At 65, Bacon had long since shot his bolt so far as his own contributions were concerned. However, from the public point of view, his death was untimely. At this very moment, another great plague was in progress—in fact, according to the meagre records of the time, the worst plague ever, killing 35,417 persons, or roughly one out of every four Londoners. As usual, no one knew quite how to handle the situation. So here again was Bacon's opportunity to impress the world with the "utility and power" of his college. Had he come forth at this time with the cause and cure of the plague as in his dream of the *New Atlantis*, no doubt he would have won more converts than by tripling his life span or, indeed, by any other scientific miracle.

However, in his *Natural History* there was nothing but a rehash of the conventional theories, and a promise of better ones in the indefinite future. In default of Bacon (and the physicians who might have profited from his contributions), all kinds of wizards, quacks, and patent medicine men came to the fore, not only on the corners of the stricken streets, but also in the palace at Whitehall. Even Buckingham (much to Bacon's horror, no doubt) now had one of these quacks on his payroll—a Dr. Lamb, described as "a conjuror and empiric." When this man's conjuring proved ineffective (it was also believed that under Buckingham's orders, he had poisoned King James), the London apprentices dragged him through the mud from Cheapside to Paul's Cross where they beat him to death with sticks and stones.

Such scenes were more appropriate to the Middle Ages than to the dawn of the new era of "man's empire over nature." Under the circumstances, Bacon and his college were hard to distinguish from any other group of discredited miracle workers. Had it not been for his past eminence as Lord Chancellor, he too might have suffered the fate of such persons. Even the publication of the *New Atlantis* the following year did not improve the situation, for the extravagance of his dream merely underscored the absence of any actual achievements. Rawley was so embarrassed by it that he added a foreword, saying that though most of the miracles Bacon had dreamed about are "within men's powers," the dream as a whole was "probably too vast."

At court, there was some ribald speculation about the fate of Gorhambury, which somehow still remained in his possession. An unknown poet wrote:

> "Now Verulam, good man, is in his grave,
> I muse who shall his house and titles have;
> That spatious, spacious, precious refectory,
> Which cost a world of wealth (so saith the story);
> Those pebble-paved brooks, empaled lakes,
> Thick clad with countless shoals of ducks and drakes."

Otherwise, no official notice was taken of Bacon's passing. At his request, his body was buried beside his mother's in little St. Michael's Church in St. Albans, not far away from his Gorhambury estate. The funeral expenses probably did not exceed £500. There was no fanfare of any kind—no orderly procession of peers and knights and companies of the city, and certainly no fine display of coaches drawn by teams of horses. Buckingham, his old protector, was too busy to attend—too busy even to open the boxes of papers that had been entrusted to him or to qualify as the executor of Bacon's will. It should be added, however, that there was not much of a will to execute. Bacon's debts now exceeded his assets by more than £15,000.

Bacon had anticipated some such finale as this, and made allowances for it. According to his will, "I bequeath my soul to God above, by the oblation of my Savior; my body to be buried obscurely. For my name and memory, I leave it to foreign nations, and to mine own countrymen, after some time be passed over." Rightly, he predicted that the quacks and anti-scientific professors would in short order be supplanted by his own followers. Until that day dawned, his little band of disciples, scattered and disorganized as they were, worked to keep his memory alive.

Out of his own pocket, his servant and kinsman by marriage, Sir Thomas Meautys, had a life size statue made, showing Bacon as he liked to remember him, sitting on a chair in his gown and hat, with his legs sprawling, his head thrown back and resting on his left forearm. This he installed over his grave in St. Michael's Church. His chaplain, Dr. Rawley, rescued the boxes and cabinets of Bacon's papers from careless executors. Thirty-one years later, when the market was favorable, he had them published along with his own memoir of the man. The Gorhambury estate passed into the hands of the above-named Meautys, who no doubt kept its gardens, ponds and other installations as well as a minor court functionary could. But after Meautys' death, the estate fell into the hands of Sir Harbottle Grimston, a man who was obviously no disciple; and Verulam House, its central shrine, was sold to a couple of carpenters for the price of the materials, a reduction from 9 or £10,000 to £400.[18] It was about this time, however, that the reinforcement of the new generation of disciples that Bacon had counted on so heartily finally began to assert themselves. In 1662, with the enthusiastic collaboration of James' grandson, King Charles II, they organized the Royal Society as the first permanent scientific college. Figuratively speaking, their first official act was to dig up Bacon's remains and rebury them with highest honors.

18   The last page of the typewritten manuscript has a portion of it torn, so there are assumptions reflected in the last couple of sentences. These include the original cost of the estate (9 or 10,000 £), and the word "heartily."

AFTERWORD

By Jamie Kemler

The author, Edgar Kemler, holds his twin sons,
Tom, left, and Jamie, at breakfast in 1959.

This book is more than 65 years in its realization. The author, my father, passed away before it was published. I was just three years old at the time of his death.

Edgar Kemler had studied philosophy at Johns Hopkins University in the mid-1930s, so I speculate that Bacon may have been a figure he had both explored and admired at that time. During his multifaceted career, my father wrote two previous books, one about the New Deal during the completion of his master's in public administration at Harvard (*The Deflation of American Ideals: An Ethical Guide for New Dealers*, 1941) and later a biography of the controversial and well-known pundit from his hometown of Baltimore, H.L. Mencken (*The Irreverent Mr. Mencken*, 1950). Along the way, he was also a Navy veteran of World War II, commanding a Landing Craft Infantry vessel in the Mediterranean Theater; a historian after the war with the U.S. Atlantic Fleet; a Washington, D.C., contributor to the *Nation* magazine; and finally a government instructor at Howard University until his death.

Publication of this work has included a transformation of my father's typewritten text on aging onionskin paper, which included his handwritten notations and edits. My review of the transcribed text in a Microsoft Word program on my laptop created an odd sensation of time travel, simulating a form of collaboration with my late father as I went back and forth between the laptop and his original draft. While this was a meaningful experience for me, it did require me and the editorial team to make judgment calls on the style on a line-by-line basis to ensure readability. So, while the core content and direction of the book reflect Professor Kemler's scholarship, the reader should know that this book is a combination of Kemler's original writing and the editors' best interpretation of that typewritten draft.

Reading his book considering the state of the world today, I am struck by its relevancy and lessons for our current society. As we approach the 400th anniversary of Bacon's death in 2026, his contributions to the scientific method and his approach for basing conclusions on evidence of true observations through experimentation have come under serious challenge, notably the recent example of COVID pandemic treatments that were never *a priori* tested. His proposal for government-sponsored research institutes and large organizations directed to discovery have many examples, spanning the Manhattan Project, as highlighted by my father; NASA's Apollo program and the James Webb telescope; the Human Genome project of the late 1990s; today's National Institutes of Health and Biomedical Advanced Research and Development Authority investments for endemic vaccine development; and the recently passed CHIPS and Science Act, which authorized over $100 billion in future government spending for scientific research and development and technology commercialization.

Francis Bacon would have been impressed at the scale his concepts had been realized.

It's difficult to imagine a time when experimentation to discover scientific advances was a novel idea, but our recent experience seems to suggest otherwise. I believe Bacon's lesson for today is that we should embrace this approach to apply to society on a global basis, to help solve our most pressing problems, among them climate change—something Bacon prophesied as he suggested opportunities to control the weather with future discoveries.

In his day, Bacon advised that universities should transition from shrines to preserve past beliefs towards engaging in research to challenge the status quo. He also foresaw technical solutions to societal challenges—suggesting that human lifespan could be extended by certain diets and understanding of human physiology. His fact-based approach was also applied to a central intelligence service for England, which he devised. He was the embodiment of a scientific visionary who also was driven by his political ambitions—in part to facilitate the establishment of his envisioned large public research efforts.

Other evidence points to a resurgence of interest in Bacon's legacy, as recent efforts in the United Kingdom to bring modern editorial theory to his voluminous work is nearing completion. The Oxford Francis Bacon Project, with eight volumes published out of twelve, will expand accessibility and allow a new generation of scholars to appreciate the wide-ranging impact of Bacon's ideas that influence science, ethics, and philosophy.

I hope that you have enjoyed my father's newly disclosed examination of the life of Francis Bacon and his influence on the world.

www.ingramcontent.com/pod-product-compliance
Lightning Source LLC
Chambersburg PA
CBHW021634120626
46545CB00002B/536